HYPNOTIC ART THERAPY

The Practitioner's Handbook

Jacquelyne Morison

Jacquelyne Morison Publishing

British Library of Cataloguing-in-Publication Data

A catalogue entry for this book is available from the British Library.

ISBN 978-0-9929973-0-4

Published in London by Jacquelyne Morison Publishing 2014 and revised and republished in 2022.

CONTENTS

ACKNOWLEDGEMENTS

I wish to acknowledge with grateful thanks the assistance of many practitioners who have so freely and willingly shared some of their experiences with me. This generosity has enabled me to provide an abundant variety of case-study material in *Hypnotic Art Therapy*.

Those practitioners who have made invaluable contributions to this book are Thérèse Allen, Sue Baker, Jennifer Bensaidane, Anne Bryson, Bradley Dearman, Max Delli Guanti, Ann Hamilton, Paul James, Sarah Long, Kerry Morgan, Lorraine Parker, Andrew Parr, Georges Philips, Lyn Philips, Jackie Reader, Roy Skinner, Sarah Stafford-Skinner, Kirsty Wick and Michelle Wolfe-Emery.

I owe an immense debt of gratitude to my professional colleagues and trainees all of whom have delighted me and, indeed, contributed to my learning process in the therapeutic equation for many years.

I am also hugely indebted to all those awe-inspiring clients whom I have helped over many years none of whom can be named but all of whom are fondly remembered.

OVERVIEW OF HYPNOTIC ART THERAPY

I became alive to new thought – to reverie peculiar in colouring. A gathering call ran among the faculties, their bugles sang, their trumpets rang an untimely summons. Imagination was roused from her rest, and she came forth impetuous and venturous.

Charlotte Brontë
Villette
1853

WHAT IS HYPNOTIC ART THERAPY?

Hypnotic Art Therapy, also known as Art Hypnotherapy, is a methodology which will allow your client to unravel his psychic stressful-traumatic experience in a creative manner by utilising imagery and symbolism in preference to the spoken word.

With Hypnotic Art Therapy your client may employ any combination of artwork, craftwork or written-work in order to access his psychic distress. Your client, therefore, can exploit any form of drawing, painting, craft-working, story-writing, poetry-writing and letter-writing. This methodology can appeal to your client particularly if he exhibits any artistic inclination although, if not, it should be clearly emphasized that no artistic skill, experience or talent will be at all necessary.

Art Hypnotherapy can be used either as a stand-alone methodology or dovetailed neatly into any psychodynamic, humanistic or cognitive practice in order to enhance your repertoire of skills and preferences.

Benefiting from Hypnotic Art Therapy

Hypnotic Art Therapy will allow your client to access non-verbal imagery and symbolism directly from the limbic system where his emotive reactions to stressful-traumatic experience reside. The primitive limbic system will hold a record of all your client's untoward experience during his lifetime which will remain locked up and troublesome until therapeutic resolution can be achieved.

With Hypnotic Art Therapy your client can, consequently, create a direct link to the source of his dilemmas without the need for speech. Frequently your client will be able to unearth his stressful-traumatic thoughts, experiences or memories, therefore, without even being conscious of what he may be releasing and resolving from his inner mind.

Once your client has unearthed his distressful psychic elements using an appropriate artwork medium he can then interpret his creative work as a means of gaining beneficial enlightenment.

Hypnotic Art Therapy may also enable your client to overcome any reluctance, avoidance, self-sabotage or resistance to the therapeutic process.

Hypnotic Art Therapy will empower your client to foster his self-expression, enhance his inherent creativity and gain a fresh perspective on life.

When working in a group environment your client may also be able to overcome any inhibitions to creative expression and enhance his skills for social interaction.

PRACTISING HYPNOTIC ART THERAPY

YOUR CLIENTELE

Hypnotic Art Therapy can be used both as a one-to-one therapy or for group therapeutic work.

Hypnotic Art Therapy will be ideal for working with children and minors or with those who do not wish to engage directly with the spoken word.

If your client exhibits a keenness for Hypnotic Art Therapy you can often find opportunities to utilise this methodology for homework assignments which can be followed up in subsequent sessions.

Essentially you may be able to render your therapeutic sessions stimulating and relaxing for your client while, simultaneously, being able to access and resolve much deeply-buried emotive distress with Hypnotic Art Therapy.

If your client is able to draw and paint then Hypnotic Art Therapy may be a logical approach for him. If your client has no experience of generating artwork then remember that he may well possess adequate design-skills which will have a significant value for him not only in the therapeutic context but also in everyday life. If your client has little or no talent in either drawing or design, however, then he should not be deterred from producing artwork because, after all, it will be the expression of his thoughts and emotive responses which will be the aim of Hypnotic Art Therapy.

MATERIALS AND EQUIPMENT

Very simple materials can be used for drawing consisting principally of paper, pens, pencils, colour pencils, felt-tipped pens and wax crayons rather than anything more elaborate in the realm of watercolours, oil paints or pastel colours. A good quality paper, such as cartridge paper, however, will often render drawn artwork more distinctive.

For poetry-writing and story-writing a simple pen and paper will, of course, suffice.

For craftwork, such as a collage, your client could be invited to supply or to collect his own materials if these are not readily available in your consulting room.

YOUR THERAPEUTIC PRACTICE

Hypnotic Art Therapy will dovetail neatly into any existing therapeutic methodology, such as dream analysis, inner child therapy, guided visualization, metaphorical imagery, therapeutic re-enactment, psychodrama, ego-state/parts therapy, age-regression, past-life regression and timeline therapy.

Hypnotic Art Therapy may also be a natural complement to other forms of creative art therapy, such as music therapy, drama therapy and dance therapy.

HYPNOTIC ART THERAPY IN PRACTICE

*Perhaps some beloved female subscriber
has arrayed an ass in the splendour and
glory of her imagination; admired his
dullness as manly simplicity; worshipped
his selfishness as manly superiority;
treated his stupidity as majestic gravity,
and used him as the brilliant fairy
Titania did a certain weaver at Athens.
I think I have seen such comedies of
errors going on in the world.*

**William Makepeace Thackeray
Vanity Fair
1847**

A TYPICAL TREATMENT STRATEGY

A typical treatment strategy for Hypnotic Art Therapy might entail a three-stage process whereby your client can select an appropriate topic, enter a hypnotic state in order to produce her creative artwork and then analyse her artwork as a means of resolving her stressful-traumatic dilemma.

The aim of Hypnotic Art Therapy will be to provide your client with a tool which she can utilise both in your consulting room and long after she has left in order to make her way in the world.

If your client wishes to continue her therapeutic process away from your consulting room then she could be assigned some artwork projects and taught self-hypnosis for this purpose.

SELECTING AN ARTWORK TOPIC

For each theme which you intend to tackle with your client using Hypnotic Art Therapy you will need to select a suitable topic on which she can work.

You may, in many cases, be able to invite your client to select a suitable topic for herself. You may, alternatively, decide to take the initiative by selecting a topic yourself for your client if you wish to give direction to her ideas. After a while you may find that your client can instigate her own topics or even voluntarily produce artwork unprompted.

If your client tends to avoid her issues or to resist the therapeutic process then she could be invited to depict her avoidance in an appropriate artwork form without actually naming this unhelpful phenomenon of circumvention.

CREATING THE ARTWORK

Once an appropriate artwork topic has been chosen you can then induce your client into a relaxed hypnotic state and encourage her to focus on the chosen topic. Even if you prefer to work with your client within a non-hypnotic methodology you can still invite her to attain a relaxed and altered state of consciousness for the purpose of utilizing Hypnotic Art Therapy.

Next you can ask your client to represent her theme in an appropriate artwork form. Your client may then spontaneously elect to draw an image, write a poem or convey a story, for instance, which relates to her chosen topic.

Often a series of artwork pieces on a given theme can be created by asking your client to relate a multiple-phase story in the form of drawn or written material.

You can, of course, discover much about your client by the way in which she creates her artwork. Your client may, for example, produce a drawing which is large with bold and vivid colours or she may draw a very tentative small-scale squiggle leaving much white space around. A drawing, therefore, may reveal much information about your client's psyche which you can grasp instantly without her having to speak a word. A poem or a story, similarly, may show hidden depths to your client's psyche and often you will be able to immediately identify the underlying message.

INTERPRETING THE ARTWORK

Once your client's artwork has been produced you can then encourage her to initiate some therapeutic discussion or dialogue. You will, by this means, be inviting your client to interpret her own artwork and to extract the therapeutic value from what she has creatively produced.

Often both the creation of the artwork and its analysis can be undertaken by your client in a hypnotic or relaxed state of mind. If your client appears to be fully conscious when she produces her artwork, however, you may easily be able to put her back into a hypnotic state of mind for interpretation and analysis purposes.

A TYPICAL TREATMENT APPROACH

You may need to plan your client's therapeutic journey in principal, at least, in order to be able to approach Hypnotic Art Therapy with a degree of confidence and understanding.

DEVISING A TREATMENT APPROACH

A typical treatment approach for Hypnotic Art Therapy would be likely to contain four elements of the therapeutic process.

PRELIMINARY PREPARATION

Initially you could utilise Hypnotic Art Therapy in order to make preliminary enquiries, assessment and preparation of your client.

INVESTIGATION AND ANALYSIS

The bulk of your Hypnotic Art Therapy programme might then proceed to enabling your client to undertake an investigative analysis of her stressful-traumatic experiences.

INHIBITION AND RESISTANCE

A trouble-shooting component of Hypnotic Art Therapy might assist your client to overcome any inhibition or resistance which could hamper her therapeutic journey.

RESOLUTION AND VALIDATION

Finally a validation stage with Hypnotic Art Therapy can allow your client to gauge how far she has travelled and, in fact, whether any further therapeutic work might be indicated.

AN OUTLINE TREATMENT APPROACH

Stage	Process
Preliminary preparation	Question and assess your client
	Identify your client's dilemmas, symptoms and disorders
	Initiate your client's therapeutic journey
	Assist your client to reach a safe-haven
Investigation and analysis	Explore your client's psyche and self-concept
	Explore your client's personal and archetypal imagery
	Work with your client's inner conflict
	Work with your client's inner child
	Work with your client's anger, fear, guilt and grief manifestations
	Work with your client's dysfunctional relationships
	Work with your client's psychosomatic-psychogenic disorders
Inhibition and resistance	Overcome your client's inhibition and therapeutic avoidance tactics
Resolution and validation	Monitor and validate your client's therapeutic progress
	Expand your client's horizons
	Assist your client to embrace the future

MONITORING A TREATMENT APPROACH

Your basic treatment strategy in outline should be monitored and then varied accordingly as your client progresses.

You can often empower your client to take the initiative in designing her own therapeutic programme once she has become accustomed to the principles of Hypnotic Art Therapy. Frequently, in practice, you will move from guiding your client completely in the early stages of her therapeutic journey to eventually allowing her ultimately to direct her own healing programme with minimal assistance from you as the facilitator.

TREATMENT TECHNIQUES

There are limitless ways in which you can encourage your client to use an artwork medium for self-investigation and self-discovery. You could, for example, ask your client to represent herself, her dilemmas and her therapeutic progress and then question her about her artwork as a means of encouraging her to look inwardly.

THE TREE OF SELF-KNOWLEDGE

You could invite your client to draw a tree and then ask her a number of questions which will stimulate her imagination and encourage her to question herself. Your client, by this means, will metaphorically reveal herself or an aspect of herself unconsciously when creating her imaginary tree.

Once your client has drawn her tree you could then pose questions such as:

Do animals play at the foot of your tree and in its branches?

Do flowers and plants grow beneath your tree?

Does your tree have a name?

Does your tree allow the birds to nest in its branches?

Does your tree bend with the wind?

Does your tree produce flowers and fruits?

Does your tree hold the secrets of the earth?

Does your tree shelter anything beneath it?

Does your tree withstand all weathers?

How old is your tree?

Is your tree a sapling?

Is your tree fully matured?

Is your tree growing in summer or in winter?

Is your tree in leaf or are its branches bare?

Is your tree tall or short?

What has your tree seen during its lifetime?

What type of tree have you drawn?

Will your tree be attacked by tree-fellers or tree-surgeons?

Will your tree live a long and healthy life?

CASE-STUDY EXAMPLE
FAMILY RESPONSIBILITIES

This client drew a sturdy oak as his Tree of Self-Knowledge assignment but, when questioned, he stated that the tree had no leaves, could bend easily with the wind and allowed no birds to nest in its branches.

From this analysis the client concluded that he showed strength to the world yet inside he felt barren, unloved and lonely. The client was then invited to investigate his feelings about himself and the pressure of his responsibilities. It transpired that others depended heavily on the client for sustenance and yet he felt inwardly pressurised because he feared being unable to deliver the goods to his family.

The client's therapeutic programme then continued to investigate his feelings of pressure from those about him in order to resolve his dilemma.

THE JOURNEY OF A LIFETIME

You could invite your client to depict a journey and then ask her a number of questions which will stimulate her imagination and encourage her to question herself. Your client, by this means, will reveal the way in which she journeys through life and the way in which she might feel about her life's voyage.

Once your client has depicted her journey you could then pose questions such as:

Are there others to help you on your journey?

Are you enjoying your travel?

Are you on foot or being carried?

Are you travelling alone or with others?

Do you like your fellow-travellers?

Do you look forward to the road ahead?

Is your journey overland, by sea or by air?

Is your journey by road or across country?

Is your journey hard or easy?

Is your journey long or short?

Is your journey straight or are there many twists and turns?

Is your journey tiring?

Is your journey uphill or downhill?

Is your means of transport comfortable and pleasurable?

Is your means of transport noisy and overcrowded?

Is your means of transport peaceful and relaxing?

Is your means of transport uncomfortable and oppressive?

What are your fellow-travellers like?

What is the weather like on your journey?

Which mode of transport are you using?

Would you like to make this journey again?

Would you like your journey to end sooner rather than later?

CASE-STUDY EXAMPLE
UNCARING MOTHER

A client drew a path through the woods as a representation of his Journey of a Lifetime assignment. When questioned the client reported that his journey was dark because his wood was dense and overgrown.

Further questioning allowed the client to appreciate that he saw his life as a welter of confusion and unhappiness because he could not find a life-partner. The client was now invited to examine his previous relationships, his associations with friends and his family relationships. This probing led the client to uncover the fact that his mother had always been cold and uncaring towards him.

The client was then invited to investigate his relationship with his mother as a means of helping him to come to terms with his past in order to move forward in life.

A DWELLING PLACE

You could invite your client to draw a dwelling place and then ask her a number of questions which will stimulate her imagination and encourage her to question herself. Your client, by this means, will reveal an aspect of her psyche, the place where she resides and whether she feels at home anywhere.

Once your client has depicted her dwelling place you could then pose questions such as:

Do you feel at home here in your dwelling place?

Do you live alone in your dwelling place?

Do you currently reside in this dwelling place?

Do you relish living with others here in this dwelling place?

Have you ever resided in this dwelling place?

How many doors does your dwelling place have?

How many windows does your dwelling place have?

Is there a good view from your dwelling place?

Is your dwelling place one which you know?

Is your dwelling place comfortable and cosy?

Is your dwelling place in a crowded city?

Is your dwelling place in a peaceful setting?

Is your dwelling place sparsely furnished or ill-equipped?

What type of dwelling place have you represented?

Where is your dwelling place located?

Would you like anyone else to live with you in your dwelling place?

Would you like anyone to leave your dwelling place?

Would you like to live alone in your dwelling place?

Would you like to live permanently in this dwelling place?

Would you like to live somewhere else?

CASE-STUDY EXAMPLE
MUGGING

This client drew a castle as her Dwelling Place assignment which was well fortified and surrounded by a moat.

The client reported that the fortification and the moat made her feel safe in her castle. The practitioner then asked the client to enumerate those times when she had not felt safe in the past. The client reported that she had been mugged in her early teens and had since then always felt unsafe.

The client's therapeutic journey now progressed to examining her feelings about the mugging and to release her emotive responses in the safe-haven of the consulting room.

WORDS AND IMAGES

You could invite your client to draw a very simple image, such as a line or a shape, and then request her to attach a word to her image. You could then encourage your client to repeat this process until a fuller picture emerges. Your client, by this means, will be able to associate any pictures in her mind with the thoughts to which they are attached.

Once your client has exhausted her repertory of words and images you could then reverse the process by asking her to write down a word and then to attach a simple image to it.

The words which your client attaches to her drawn images will, of course, allow her to reveal to herself what lies beneath the surface of her mind. You will obviously learn much about your client from this therapeutic procedure according to the nature of her drawn images. A square, for example, might indicate rigidity while a nebulous shape might convey flexibility. A large bold image or a small tentative drawing may similarly indicate your client's personality traits or her view of herself.

CASE-STUDY EXAMPLE
CANINE PHOBIA

This client drew a jagged circle as her first image and attached the word "Help" to this shape as her Words and Images assignment. The client then drew a square to which she attached the word "Rescue" followed by a star-shape which she associated with the phrase "Dog barking".

Apparently the client had been frightened by a loudly barking dog when she was a young child going home from school. The client explained that her mother had not collected her from school one day. When going home alone the client had then encountered this frightening animal and had developed a canine phobia from that time.

The client was now invited to imaginatively question her own mother about the time when she was not there for the child.

> *The client was then invited to utilise therapeutic re-enactment and inner child rescue methodology in order to reprimand her mother and thereby alleviate her fear of dogs.*

TELLING A STORY

You could invite your client to build up a picture gradually in the form of a story which has episodes or chapters.

You might start by asking your client to draw a simple image, write a single word or write a single phrase as her starting-point.

You could then request that your client describe her image, word or phrase in order to elaborate her thinking as the first chapter of her story.

You could then tell your client that she needs to develop her story by producing a second image, word or phrase which, in some way, extends or clarifies the first chapter of her tale.

Again your client could be requested to outline the thinking behind her second chapter as a corollary of the first.

You could then invite your client to repeat the process for any subsequent chapters until a fuller picture emerges which can initiate therapeutic discussion and self-discovery.

The advantage of using a narrative-oriented methodology will be to enable your client to build up a picture gradually step-by-step. With each step your client will frequently not be able to predict the outcome and, therefore, she will be working directly from her unconscious mind rather than with her intellect.

CASE-STUDY EXAMPLE
NEGLECTFUL PARENTS

This client began her Telling a Story assignment by producing a drawing of a mouse. The client explained that the mouse represented her father who was never able to stand up to her mother and his mother-in-law.

The client then wrote the word "Hateful" which she explained was the way in which she felt about her mother and her maternal grandmother who were always criticizing her.

Next the client drew a picture of two elephants and she explained that these animals represented her mother and her grandmother who had metaphorically trampled all over her when she was a growing child.

Finally the client drew a picture of a river which she explained was there to drown both her parents and her grandmother who had not been there for her as a child because they were all working out their own angst. The client, by this means, had told the story of her childhood and had also worked out creatively how she could rescue herself unprompted by the practitioner.

OPPOSING ASPECTS

You could invite your client to consider various opposing aspects of her life or differing elements of her psyche by asking her to depict and then to define one or more images in juxtaposition. Your client could, for instance, be encouraged to represent her opposing aspects pictorially and then asked to describe each component.

Your client could initially be asked to represent two opposing elements of her psyche which are in conflict. Your client could then be requested to describe or to elaborate on these two disparate elements as a means of noting the tension and conflict between each. If your client, for example, believes herself to be alternately happy and sad, or if she feels brave one moment and timid the next, then this dynamic relationship can be depicted in an artwork form. You can, in this way, utilise some form of parts therapy or ego-state methodology with your client.

Your client could also be invited to depict three differing elements of herself, her life or her dilemmas as a means of allowing her to discover any three-way tensions. Using three variant aspects could permit your client to gain a new perspective on the way in which she might view life from a healthy dynamic rather than from a black-and-white standpoint.

You could, similarly, use multiple opposing aspects of four or more elements in order to encourage your client to see her troubles from many different angles. A group of aspects of even-numbered images may inform you of the stability of your client's thinking while an odd-numbered group of aspects may encourage her to think in a more fluid manner.

The advantage of using this kind of methodology will be to empower your client to consider herself and her life from many different and dynamic viewpoints in order to extract the essence from each.

CASE-STUDY EXAMPLE
INSOMNIA

A client was requested to draw multiple aspects of herself and her dilemma as part of her Opposing Aspects assignment for self-discovery.

The client drew a picture of a nightmare, a sleepwalker, a stormy sea, a cloud and a sleeping child.

The client then explained that when she suffered from insomnia she felt that the next day was merely a sleep-walking nightmare because she had been deprived of rest the night before.

When lying awake the client was inclined to worry about the next day and to envisage being under par at work.

The client, therefore, believed that her nights were a nightmare because of her insomnia, that she would become a sleep-walker in the daytime and that she was generally being tossed about on a stormy sea because of her troubles as depicted in her first three illustrations.

The client also imagined, on the positive side, that there was within her an ability to rest and to float on a cloud as she went off to sleep as if she were a child as represented by the last two aspects of herself.

The client's therapeutic journey now proceeded to investigate those times in her life when she had felt continually worried, concerned about the next day and beset by heavy responsibilities.

The client then recalled times when at school she had been terrorised by an over-strict teacher who had insisted that she do an inordinate amount of additional homework because she had been a very promising pupil. The client had then developed insomnia because she was constantly worried about her performance at school the next day.

The client was, in this way, able to overcome her insomnia because she had identified the root cause of her trouble and had found a means of settling the score with her unhelpful teacher.

PRELIMINARY PREPARATION

*It is his companion all this evening, his
solace, his delight. It opens his designs to
his family, it introduces you among
them, it diffuses through the party those
pleasantest feelings of our nature, eager
curiosity and warm prepossession. How
cheerful, how animated, how suspicious,
how busy their imaginations all are.*

Emma
Jane Austen
1815

CLIENT ENQUIRIES

A starting-point for your client's therapeutic journey will usually be to question, assess and observe him in terms of his symptomatic patterns and his character traits in order to determine the way in which you could help him to approach his healing journey.

Preliminary questioning and assessment of your client may also constitute a means of introducing him to Hypnotic Art Therapy. Your client could be asked, for instance, to depict his presenting symptoms, what he feels about the prospect of his therapeutic journey and what he hopes to achieve in his sessions.

CLIENT QUESTIONING

By carefully questioning your client at the outset you will be introducing him to the way in which he could unearth his problems and find ways of resolving his dilemmas. By asking your client to focus on his presenting problems as the effect of his underlying dilemmas you can concurrently allow him to indirectly access the root cause. Your client, in this way, you will be utilizing the effect as the means of arriving at the cause wherein resolution can take place.

You will need typically to question your client about his problems, background, status and lifestyle all of which will be fodder for artwork topics.

SUGGESTED CLIENT QUESTIONING TOPICS

Behavioural motivations and repetitive patterns

Beliefs and convictions

Childhood and adulthood stressful-traumatic experience

Education and schooling

Intimate and casual relationships

Leisure activities

Occupation and status

Previous experience of therapeutic intervention

Prospect of therapeutic intervention

Psychological and physiological health

Supplements and medication

CLIENT ASSESSMENT

You will need typically to assess your client at the inception of his therapeutic programme in order to gauge his suitability for therapeutic intervention. This information can usually be gleaned either by judicial questioning or merely via your intuitive observation.

Once you have a clear picture of your client's psyche and personality traits you will then be in an ideal position to design his therapeutic strategy. You will also be well equipped to assist him if he attempts to avoid any fundamental issues which he might need to address.

SUGGESTED CLIENT ASSESSMENT TOPICS

Communication ability

Emotive reactions and self-expression

Learning and cognitive ability

Life-circumstances

Motivation and life-purpose

Outlook and practical reality

Personal traits

Reaction to you as the practitioner

Self-image and appearance

CLIENT OBSERVATION

As your client begins to travel along his therapeutic path it may be wise for you to observe and monitor him as an individual within the therapeutic context. Your intuitive observation, of course, will allow you to assess the extent of your client's dilemmas and his potential for therapeutic resolution.

Your client may be too close to his own psychic state and his work with you to be able to take an objective overview of where he came from and where he may be going. As an impartial observer, therefore, you can take a neutral stance when making decisions about your client.

SUGGESTED CLIENT OBSERVATION TOPICS

Degree of relaxation in your presence

Degree of trust in your ability as a practitioner

Extent of compliance or non-compliance

Future optimism

Progress since initial consultation

Transference manifestations

Willingness to strive for personal goals

Willingness to take responsibility for personal progress

CASE-STUDY EXAMPLE
MY LIFE'S JOURNEY

A client sought therapeutic intervention because she felt that her life had hitherto been beset by troubles which she wanted to shelve.

The client explained that her children had recently left home and that this event presented an ideal opportunity for her to make some radical lifestyle changes.

The client, however, felt that she needed to let go of some tragedies from the past before she could move forward. The client was hence asked to depict her past and current life and to illustrate the way in which she viewed her future.

The client produced a drawing which showed her children with their past and ongoing troubles.

The client reported that one of her daughters had been in an unhappy relationship which had ended in financial disaster for her. Another daughter was out of work and the client's son seemed very angry with his mother for no apparent reason. The client's three children, therefore, were illustrated along a winding path which led to the present.

The client also saw herself in her picture as a young and innocent child who had no idea of what being a mother would entail. The client reported, moreover, that her husband seemed little concerned with her predicament and those of her children, either now or in the past, which meant that she had borne the entire burden of these upheavals alone.

The client, however, saw her future path in terms of a number of available options. The client, for instance, was considering moving house, doing some voluntary work, visiting her grandchildren more frequently and taking up dressmaking as a hobby.

In this client's first artwork piece, therefore, she had portrayed her entire existence which the problems of having a family had generated while, on the other hand, she had depicted her own optimism about the future. The client thus needed simply to talk through her past troubles and to find a way of coping with her current difficulties.

The practitioner was able to use the client's drawing as a clue not only to the starting-point for her investigative therapy but also as a means of planning her therapeutic programme.

The practitioner then proceeded to work with the client's inner child who was able to speak about life long ago and the way in which she was ill-prepared to face the reality of the future as a mother. Once the client had addressed these intrepid issues she was then able to move forward and to plan her own future as an adult. The client realised, of course, that as a very young child she had been ill-equipped to face the future but, as an adult, she was now much stronger and wiser.

EXPLORING DILEMMAS

Your client could be asked to depict his presenting stressful-traumatic dilemmas in an appropriate artwork medium as his introduction to the therapeutic environment. Your client could be asked to represent his symptoms, his emotive reactions, his behavioural tendencies, his motivation and his life-situation, for instance, as a way of introducing him to his therapeutic sessions.

Often your client will be able to depict his dilemmas in life quite easily and unaided but, at other times, you may need to coax him towards identifying his perceived difficulties. Mind exploration in connection with unclear or confusing issues or symptomatic patterns can, of course, usually be easily achieved by your client with the aid of a hypnotic trance state.

By inviting your client to generate artwork for his presenting dilemmas you will be aiming to move him from having a cognitive appreciation of his troubles to a much deeper level of understanding and enlightenment. When your client explores stressful-traumatic dilemmas, therefore, this will assist him to appreciate the nature of his presenting symptomatic patterns as well as the likely cause.

Once your client has outlined his symptomatic patterns and been familiarised with the therapeutic process he can then be invited to examine those issues which need to be addressed.

Your client's distress may change naturally in the course of his therapeutic programme and, therefore, you might need to return to his dilemmas at a later stage in order to evaluate his progress.

SUGGESTED TOPICS FOR EXPLORING DILEMMAS

My difficulties and challenges

My gains and losses

My positives and negatives

My scales and balances

My successful and unsuccessful projects

My unfinished business

My unhappy relationships

My uphill and downhill struggles

My worries and distresses

HYPNOTIC TEXT EXAMPLE

Exploring dilemmas

Allow yourself to relax and focus on your feelings of distress and trouble.

Just clear your mind of other notions and allow yourself to submerge your thinking with that idea of the distress which has brought you here today.

Let your mind settle on the troubles you have spoken about today and the impact which such distress may be having on your life. Look also at the situations which have caused your dilemmas and the feelings which underpin them.

Perhaps select the scene which most attracts your attention and let that filter through your mind. Study each person in that scene in detail and allow yourself to understand your reactions and your emotions. The more you can feel your feelings the more you will be able to understand your own distress and to expel your unwanted reactions.

In a moment or two I am going to ask you to draw a simple picture or to write a short poem which represents what you are thinking about so that you can record your distress in a pictorial or written form.

> *I am not at all asking you to produce an artistic masterpiece or to write a poem which scans but just something very simple which depicts your thoughts and feelings.*
>
> *Know, in your own mind, that you can easily tap into this form of inherent creativity without any adverse judgement or criticism of yourself.*
>
> *Absolutely no talent or skill or experience will be at all necessary here in this safe and healing place.*
>
> *When you have gathered your thoughts and when you are quite ready, therefore, perhaps you would like to pick up your artwork materials and talk to yourself in this natural way.*

CASE-STUDY EXAMPLE
GETTING LOST IN LIFE

This client suffered from indecision and was uncertain about making a career-move.

The client reported that he had been offered promotion in his job but had, simultaneously, been looking elsewhere because he had become somewhat disenchanted with his current employer. The client was, therefore, at an important crossroads in his life and sought therapeutic intervention in order to help him with this decision.

The client also confessed that he was unhappy with his current partner with whom he had been living for several years. This situation also added to the client's dilemma of indecision and his feeling of being lost and trapped.

The client was, consequently, invited to depict his indecision and the accompanying emotive effect.

The client was able to represent his hesitancy and his uncertainty in the form of a perilous tightrope along which he showed himself at various stages in his life.

The illustration which the client generated was entitled "Getting lost in life".

The client was now requested to interpret his picture of "Getting lost in life".

The client spoke about how his life had drifted when he was a child and when he was at school.

The client reported that he and his mother had moved several times during his childhood and that, therefore, he was forced to change schools many times. These constant upheavals meant that the client had been unable to settle anywhere and to make permanent friends.

The client also spoke of his unhappiness because he had been an only child and he very seldom saw his father. His relationship with his mother was fairly satisfactory but the client felt aggrieved because his father had always been cold and distant both physically and metaphorically.

The client was then invited to revisit those occasions when he had felt this unhappiness, loneliness and isolation and to discuss his emotive reactions. The client was thus able to release his pent-up emotions as a means of freeing himself from the past.

After a few sessions the client reported seeing the future more clearly and feeling less unsettled. The client was then able to plan his future both in terms of his work and his partner.

The client subsequently elected to accept the promotion he had been offered at work and, somewhat reluctantly, he decided to leave his partner and to gain some personal freedom.

STARTING A THERAPEUTIC JOURNEY

Often you will need to introduce your client to the idea of a therapeutic voyage of self-discovery. This tactic will be particularly important if your client is a newcomer to the process of therapeutic self-exploration.

When using this approach you will be able to gauge the extent of your client's commitment to his therapeutic journey and his degree of optimism or pessimism about his ability to progress and ultimately to recover. You may also be able to allay any misconceptions which your client may harbour about the role of therapeutic intervention and his role in the therapeutic equation.

If your client can be compliant and determined as a therapeutic seeker this notion will usually be depicted as a forward-looking journey. If your client, conversely, might be likely to scupper his own efforts at therapeutic investigation then, as an avoider, he may well portray his journey as an uphill struggle.

SUGGESTED TOPICS FOR STARTING A THERAPEUTIC JOURNEY

A bird's flight

A bridge to recovery

A countryside walk

A fairground ride

A journey through the changing seasons

A magic-carpet ride

A path of mystery

A path through a maze

A puzzle requiring a solution

A sea voyage

A treasure hunt

Hypnotic text example

> ## *Starting the therapeutic journey*
>
> *Perhaps you can think of your work with me in terms of a special journey which you are undertaking for your own benefit?*
>
> *Maybe your voyage will take you through the countryside or by the sea, along a winding path or down a long tunnel? You might, for instance, see yourself walking through a woodland glade with the sun shafting through the trees and making patterns on the ground beneath you. You might also notice some little furry creatures darting around you, hear the birds singing and listen to the crackle of leaves and twigs beneath your feet as you walk. Perhaps a stream may follow your path or a bird will show you the way ahead?*
>
> *Travel onward, uphill and down dale, with that feeling of optimism in your soul. Notice also whether the weather is bright or dreary and observe how frequently it changes as you journey onwards. You may, of course, not always see the path ahead of you because of inclement weather and you may not always be able to see what might be round the next bend or the next twist in the road.*
>
> *Just allow yourself to travel at your own pace and in your own way.*
>
> *Then, perhaps, in a moment or two, you can depict the scenery around you on your voyage as if you were telling the story of your life's journey and the road ahead in your own special way?*
>
> *When you are ready, therefore, you can just gently open your eyes and show me in an artwork form of your choice what you have been thinking about on your journey, what you have experienced and what might lie ahead.*

CASE-STUDY EXAMPLE
PROSPECT OF THERAPY

A client was invited to depict her view of her therapeutic journey by creating a drawing of what she imagined it might constitute.

This client chose to show her journey from childhood to the present and then into the future. The client, in effect, produced a time-line image of her life's journey.

At the start of her journey the client saw herself as a young child with a skipping rope who was alone in the playground at school.

The client then explained that she viewed her therapeutic voyage as a means of reaching a path which would allow her to blossom in life.

The brown line in the client's picture showed a sub-route with a connecting link to the main path.

The client's main path was represented in green as the colour of plenty. Once on this path the client could then progress in life until she blossomed as a flower with many opportunities for advancement.

The client reported that she wished to open up her life and to seek out new possibilities both in her social life and at work. The red, blue and brown branches at the top of the client's main path represented the various avenues which she was hoping to explore in the future.

This client, therefore, depicted not only where she was now but also showed her optimism about reaching and realizing her goals. This client proved to her practitioner, therefore, that she was ready and willing to undertake her therapeutic journey.

The client's journey then began with an investigation of her childhood and how her inner child had felt when she was alone in the school-playground.

REACHING A SAFE-HAVEN

The concept of a safe-haven can usually be easily depicted by your client in an artwork form. The safe-haven image can then be utilised by your client whenever the going might get tough in life.

Your aim should be to invite your client to portray a safe place in which he can share his thoughts and feelings with you even though some may be unpleasant. Your client could, for example, be requested to choose a suitable sanctuary or a safe harbour when he rides life's stormy seas.

SUGGESTED TOPICS FOR REACHING A SAFE-HAVEN

A castle

A cave

A cellar

A deep recess

A desert island

A house

A private room

A protective cloak

A secret garden

A spiritual retreat

An attic

An auric light

An oasis

The countryside

HYPNOTIC TEXT EXAMPLE

Reaching a safe-haven

If at any time along your therapeutic path you would like to seek sanctuary and to escape from the outside world just know, in your inner mind, that this will be entirely possible for you at any stage.

You could, for example, see yourself on a desert island or in a secret garden where no-one can reach you.

Perhaps you can see a cave on the beach or a spiritual retreat in which you can gain much-needed warmth, comfort and nourishment for yourself?

Maybe an enchanted fairyland will be your ideal location as a healing sanctuary?

In this special place you will be far from the madding crowd and alone with your own thoughts. Here no-one can make demands on you or expect anything from you. You can be completely protected from all those who might disturb you in the normal course of your life.

You can now simply be yourself.

Make this retreat your own special place where you know that all will be well whenever you come here.

See this place in vivid detail because, in a moment or two, I am going to ask you to show me what this special place for you looks like and where you are right now.

Notice how this safe and special place makes you feel and how it can afford you great comfort and then, whenever you are ready, you can simply begin to reproduce your image nice and slowly and gently and in your own time.

CASE-STUDY EXAMPLE
WORK STRESS

A client whose stress-levels at work were extremely high was asked to depict his safe-haven as a means of allowing himself space to get away from it all in the therapeutic context.

This client reported that he was continually being harassed by his work colleagues both in the office and even at home. The client found it difficult, therefore, to maintain boundaries and to deflect interruptions to his home-life.

The client's partner and family also felt invaded by his work colleagues and, therefore, difficulties were arising at home as well as at work.

This client produced an illustration which depicted a safe-haven to which he felt he could retreat when necessary.

The client was, of course, invited to address his boundary issues but was always encouraged to use his safe-haven imagery in order to remind himself that he could achieve sanctuary whenever necessary in his daily life.

INVESTIGATION AND ANALYSIS

There were two images – two living forms that tore her heart in two, as if it had been the heart of a mother who seems to see her child divided by the sword, and presses one bleeding half to her breast while her gaze goes forth in agony towards the half which is carried away by the lying woman that has never known the mother's pang.

**Middlemarch
George Eliott
1869**

EXPLORING THE PSYCHE

Your client may need to take a long hard look at herself in the therapeutic context. You could, for this reason, begin your client's therapeutic exploration by asking her to represent herself, her view of the world and her role in life in an artwork form. You could, moreover, invite your client to explore her psyche in terms of her self-concept, self-image and her place in the world as she sees it.

EXPLORING THE SELF-CONCEPT

Essentially if you can obtain your client's own view of herself you will be gaining a direct access into her psyche. Your client could, for example, reveal her self-image or gauge whether she feels herself to be a worthy person. Your client, by this route, will access her inner feelings of guilt, shame or failure.

SUGGESTED TOPICS FOR EXPLORING THE SELF-CONCEPT

A self-advertisement

An ideal me

I am

My beliefs and convictions

My childhood, adolescence and maturity

My likes and dislikes

My loves and hates

My positive and negative self

My social mask or persona

Who am I?

EXPLORING SOCIAL INTERACTION

Your client will constantly be exposed to the social world which may present many difficulties for her which might need to be explored in the therapeutic context. Your client, for instance, could be requested to portray herself in her daily life, how she goes about the world and what she thinks of others. Your client could also be invited to examine her own emotive responses and motivational reactions to others.

SUGGESTED TOPICS FOR EXPLORING SOCIAL INTERACTION

At work, at play and at home

Attending a fancy-dress party

Attending an auction

Exploring my costume wardrobe

Me and others

My place in the world

My role in life

Opening a treasure-chest

Opening books in a library

The chapters of my life

Visiting a car-boot sale

Visiting a toy-shop

Visiting an art exhibition

Watching a carnival

Watching a masquerade

Watching a puppet-show

Watching the world go by

HYPNOTIC TEXT EXAMPLE

Exploring yourself

Maybe you can take the opportunity now to look closely at yourself? Who are you, I wonder? What do you think about yourself?

What do you think about the person you are? Do you feel that you are wise or stupid? Do you believed that you are good-looking or plain, beautiful or ugly? Would you wish to be taller or shorter or thinner or fatter? Do you think you are kind and caring or selfish and unfeeling? Do you feel that you are accomplished or inadequate? Are you a success or a failure in life?

Do you, in fact, like the way you are now?

Are you proud of yourself? Are you kind to yourself or a hard task-master with yourself? How harshly do you judge yourself? Take time now to consider how you feel about the person you believe yourself to be knowing that you will receive no judgement here in this safe place.

What might you also think about your place in the world? Do you consider yourself to be outgoing and sociable or shy and retiring? Are you comfortable with people or do you feel awkward in the presence of others? How might you be at a business meeting or at an interview perhaps? Do you avoid going out because you might bump into someone you do not wish to meet? Do you, in fact, shun any form of confrontation? Are you the life and soul of the party or are you the wallflower cowering in the corner?

Perhaps you are not at all a social animal but merely a loner who would like to live in a world of your own free from the pressures of having to cope with others?

> *How do you view the way in which you might come across to others? Do you long to be able to buy expensive clothes and jewellery just to be one step ahead of the rest? Would you like to be driving a faster and more impressive car? Would you wish to live in a bigger house in a posh district so that you can tell all your friends? Would you like to be mixing with the upper set?*
>
> *Spend some time considering who you are, how you see yourself and how you interact with others because soon it will be time to take up your writing or drawing materials and portray these notions.*
>
> *When you can talk to yourself in this way, of course, you will really be coming to grips with your inner mind and the way in which you tick as a person.*

CASE-STUDY EXAMPLE
FAILURE SYNDROME

> *This client saw himself as someone who had been a failure for most of his life.*
>
> *The client spoke initially about the way in which he had failed several examinations at school or he had not done as well as had been expected of him.*
>
> *Because of his so-called failures at school the client then felt that he had let other people down. This situation naturally had a knock-on effect for the client when he went out to work.*
>
> *The client was, accordingly, invited to illustrate his feelings of failure.*
>
> *The client produced a drawing which showed his childhood home which appeared conventional on the outside but, on the inside, there were constant rows and fights between his parents.*

Apparently the client had been so troubled by the conflict at home that this concern had spilled over into his schoolwork. When the client was at school, therefore, his concentration-levels had been minimal because of his preoccupation with the strife at home.

The client also reported that finding work without any appropriate qualifications was a problematic area for him. The client was very intelligent but, in the workplace, his job was mundane and far beneath his abilities. It was as if the client's low-paid and menial work reflected his self-concept.

His childhood issues were then discussed at length in the therapeutic context in order to allow the client to come to terms with the past and to build some confidence.

The client was also able to realise the adverse consequences of his extremely unhappy childhood and this enlightenment, in itself, allowed him to start anew.

Once free from the anguish of the past the client was then able to take constructive action about qualifying as a teacher of English as a foreign language. The client had enjoyed English and foreign language studies at school but his lack of application had prevented him from taking this option further at the time.

Through therapeutic investigation, therefore, the client now became clear about his path forward in life.

CASE-STUDY EXAMPLE
TEARS BEHIND THE SMILEY FACE

This client stated that she suffered from despair and downheartedness but was initially reluctant to talk about her feelings.

The client was encouraged, consequently, to draw her thoughts instead as a ploy for dislodging her hesitancy.

The client produced a picture which showed a happy and smiley face in the form of a mask which she wore when she went out into the world. This face did not, of course, represent the client's true self because inside she felt constantly on the verge of tears as represented by the small child beside the mask.

The client explained that she would feel dreadful inside and would often hide away from the world by not venturing out unless absolutely necessary. When the client had to visit the shops, for instance, she would smile and be extremely jolly with all those whom she met.

The client also reported that she would become the life and soul of any social gathering which she attended with so-called friends, particularly when her depressive moods were at their height, but confessed that inwardly she felt embarrassed by such behaviour. The client was, of course, acutely aware of the sheer pretence of her actions but currently felt powerless to change.

The client, however, stated that she would always have to pay for the efforts she made to maintain her front by collapsing when she returned home.

After a party or a social gathering the client would often have to spend some days at home and often in bed because of her unhappiness in order to recover from the excitement and enforced effort of social interaction.

The client also felt that other people saw her as a happy and carefree person but she was terrified that anyone would discover her true feelings of despondency.

The client was invited to consider her childhood days and to explore her life-long feelings of despair.

The client then spoke about having a mother who always insisted on being the focus of attention and would not tolerate any deflection of the spotlight. Her mother, therefore, became very demanding of her daughter and the client, consequently, grew to resent her parent for her selfishness and her neglect of her maternal duty.

The client was then asked to depict this unhappy situation in a graphic form.

The client drew a picture of her mother as the limelight-seeker and herself as the deprived and unloved child.

By creating this image the client now began to understand the impact which her mother's attention-seeking ways had on her as a young child.

The client clearly saw that because her mother had been selfish she had, as a child, lacked the love which she craved as her birthright.

The client then elected to represent in an artwork form the way in which she could get even with her mother for the injustice of her childhood.

The client thus undertook a form of therapeutic re-enactment for herself as her means of settling the score with her mother in graphic and imaginative terms.

The client showed herself as a small child with other imaginary helpers around her. The client's helpers then wreaked vengeance on her mother in the form of a series of thunderbolts. The client's mother was now bent double with remorse as she was forced to accept her punishment.

The client noticed that her mother had become smaller in her picture and that she herself had become more powerful with the creation of her imaginary helpers. The client was now invited tc assume the power and the strength of her helpers as a means of moving forward in life.

Once the client had shed tears and had released her resentment she then began to recover from her difficulties, to gain more personal confidence and to act more normally on social occasions.

The client also reported, at her next session, that her despondent moods had considerably lifted as a result of her therapeutic exploration and resolution.

CASE-STUDY EXAMPLE
HIDING FROM THE WORLD

This client felt that she was unable to be herself in the social world.

The client maintained that she constantly wore a mask when meeting or interacting with others particularly when socializing or at work.

The client described the way in which she continually felt the need to please others and was afraid of those whom she believed were much wiser or more accomplished.

The client reported that she was also scared that she would put on the wrong mask one day when she met someone and that her friends or colleagues would meet, talk about her and compare notes about her reactions to others.

The practitioner then questioned the client about her social mask and from this probing it transpired that she not only wore a mask but also adopted a complete costume wardrobe for each person whom she encountered.

The client, therefore, was invited to depict her costume wardrobe in a graphic form.

When asked to analyse her drawing the client realised that she was frequently playing the clown as a means of disappearing into the background while remaining in the foreground. The client saw herself in this drawing as being a faceless non-entity who was afraid of the world at large.

The client's therapeutic journey then began to focus on the fears behind her costumes and her masks.

EXPLORING SYMBOLIC IMAGERY

Hypnotic Art Therapy lends itself naturally to an exploration of your client's symbolic imagery.

Your client may wish to explore the symbolic imagery which has a personal significance or a particular meaning for her. Your client may also feel inclined to explore some relevant archetypal imagery because of the cultural significance of symbolism which can be universally recognised and interpreted accordingly.

PERSONAL SYMBOLISM

Your client will possess her own personal symbolic imagery which will retain its particular significance for her alone as an individual. Your client may, therefore, identify herself with an object, an animal, an imaginary being or a given role-model.

When working with your client it will nearly always be important for you to allow her to access her own personal symbolism as this can often be portrayed very accurately in an artwork form. Your client's personal symbolism, inevitably, will frequently be the key to accessing her innermost psyche.

SUGGESTED TOPICS FOR EXPLORING PERSONAL SYMBOLISM

My astrological sign

My dreams and nightmares

My hopes and aspirations

My key to existence

My Pandora's box

My schooldays

My shamanic power-animal

My special friend

My special retreat

My spirit-guide

My undiscovered planet

My universe

The end of my rainbow

The sun clouds and the rain clouds

UNIVERSAL SYMBOLISM

Your client will not live in isolation from her social world and, therefore, the archetypal symbolism which depicts that cultural environment will hold a special significance for her.

Your client, for instance, will recognise the symbolism behind the superhero, the superstar, the business tycoon and the catwalk model. Your client may also identify with the concept of a lucky charm, a magic wand, a lottery win, a fast car and an internet profile as universal archetypal messages.

Your client will be a crazy mixture of her inner and outer world, her life's experience and her future potential all of which will interact to form her unique psyche. When appropriate, therefore, your client could be invited to reproduce a mandala symbol in order to depict her personal elements, influencing factors and emotive reactions in symbolic form.

Carl Jung recognised that the mandala symbol, as a divided circle, can provide the key to your client's psyche because it is an archetypal symbol which can represent the diverse elements of the mind. Your client's mind, for instance, will contain her emotive reactions, her responses to the world about her and those external circumstances which might influence her motivation both consciously and unconsciously. The symbol of the mandala, therefore, can be considered as representative of your client's conscious social interaction, her externalised motivation and any way in which she might progress in the outer world. The mandala symbol may also depict your client's inner imaginative, dreamlike and fantasy-oriented life in the realm of the unconscious mind.

PSYCHIC SYMBOLISM

<table>
<tr><td colspan="3">

CONSCIOUS MIND

Externalised behaviours & motivations
Externalised thoughts & actions
Extrovert & introvert personality traits
Objective reality
Over-developed & under-developed faculties
Progression in life

</td></tr>
<tr><td>

Outer influences and circumstances

</td><td>

TRUE SELF

</td><td>

Inner influences and experiences

</td></tr>
<tr><td colspan="3">

UNCONSCIOUS MIND

Cognitive processes
Creativity & intuition
Dreams & imagination
Genetic history
Innate intelligence
Instinctive & survivalist reactions
Memories
Motivation
Perception
Subjective reality
Unresolved stress-trauma manifestation

</td></tr>
</table>

SUGGESTED TOPICS FOR EXPLORING ARCHETYPAL IMAGERY

A black sheep

A damsel in distress

A guardian angel

A hero or a superstar

A knight in shining armour

A public figure

A ship on the horizon

A spinning wheel

A wise oracle

Jack and the giant

Mars and Venus

Sleeping beauty

HYPNOTIC TEXT EXAMPLE

Exploring symbolic imagery

We are surrounded by symbols, images and icons in our lives. We see shapes all about us.

We take hold of the concept of these shapes and forms and then interpret them according to our own reference-points.

We see the fluffy, billowing clouds forming in the sky. We watch the waves making shapes in the sea which stretches right out to the horizon and beyond. We notice the outline of the landscape and the cityscape.

We know the shape of human beings, animals and flowers and can recognise these objects by their unique silhouette.

We then attribute symbolic meaning to these forms in many ways.

We all understand what is meant by a superstar or a superhero. We all know that fat cats live in big houses. Most of us know our astrological sign. We all know that a butterfly flits from flower to flower. We think of the rose as a sweet flower while its thorn can damage and destroy.

Some of these symbols are commonly recognised by all of us but others are unique and individual. We all have our personal set of symbols which we regard as our very own and not the property of anyone else.

You might think of yourself as being as happy as a playful bunny or as curious as an inquisitive squirrel.

You might believe yourself to be encased within a black cloud on a rainy day.

You might also think of yourself as either a tower of strength or a quivering jelly.

You may seem to be an eager beaver or a lazy bones.

The most important symbols, therefore, are those which apply to you alone and you are the only person who can create and recognise your own individual signs and symbols. It will be as if your symbolism might be the only thing which you can claim as your own.

Perhaps you could now focus in on your own personal symbolism or those symbols which are representative of the ideas which we all possess in our culture?

In a moment, therefore, I shall ask you to depict any images which will come from your own mind spontaneously as being relevant for you and your dilemmas. And when you are really ready perhaps you can just gently show me what you are thinking about now?

CASE-STUDY EXAMPLE
STARTING A BUSINESS

This client sought therapeutic assistance because she felt a lack of motivation about starting her own business. The client wished to open a children's nursery, had completed her training and had the capital to launch the business but felt inexplicably blocked within herself.

When the client was questioned about what was stopping her from taking the first step she replied that there was no obvious reason. It transpired that she had spent much time planning and preparing to launch her business but, when it came to the crunch, she felt that she was holding herself back for no apparent reason.

When asked what she might need to launch her project the client replied that she needed some outside assistance from a spiritual source. The client was, consequently, invited to depict her way of gaining some spiritual inspiration in an artwork form. Because the client had stated that she regularly meditated within a spiritual development group she was asked to meditate for one week in order to find her spiritual guidance and to represent this assistance in an appropriate manner.

The client first wrote a poem as her way of asking the cosmos to provide her with the assistance which she needed in order to begin her project.

A nursery place

By all the powers of existence that be

Please deliver help to me

Send me a creature, man or beast,

Who can allow me to start up, at least.

I can make a happy place

To help the children into grace.

At her next session the client drew a picture of her newly-discovered spirit-guide. This spiritual helper was, in fact, an angelic being whom the client had seen in her mind for some time.

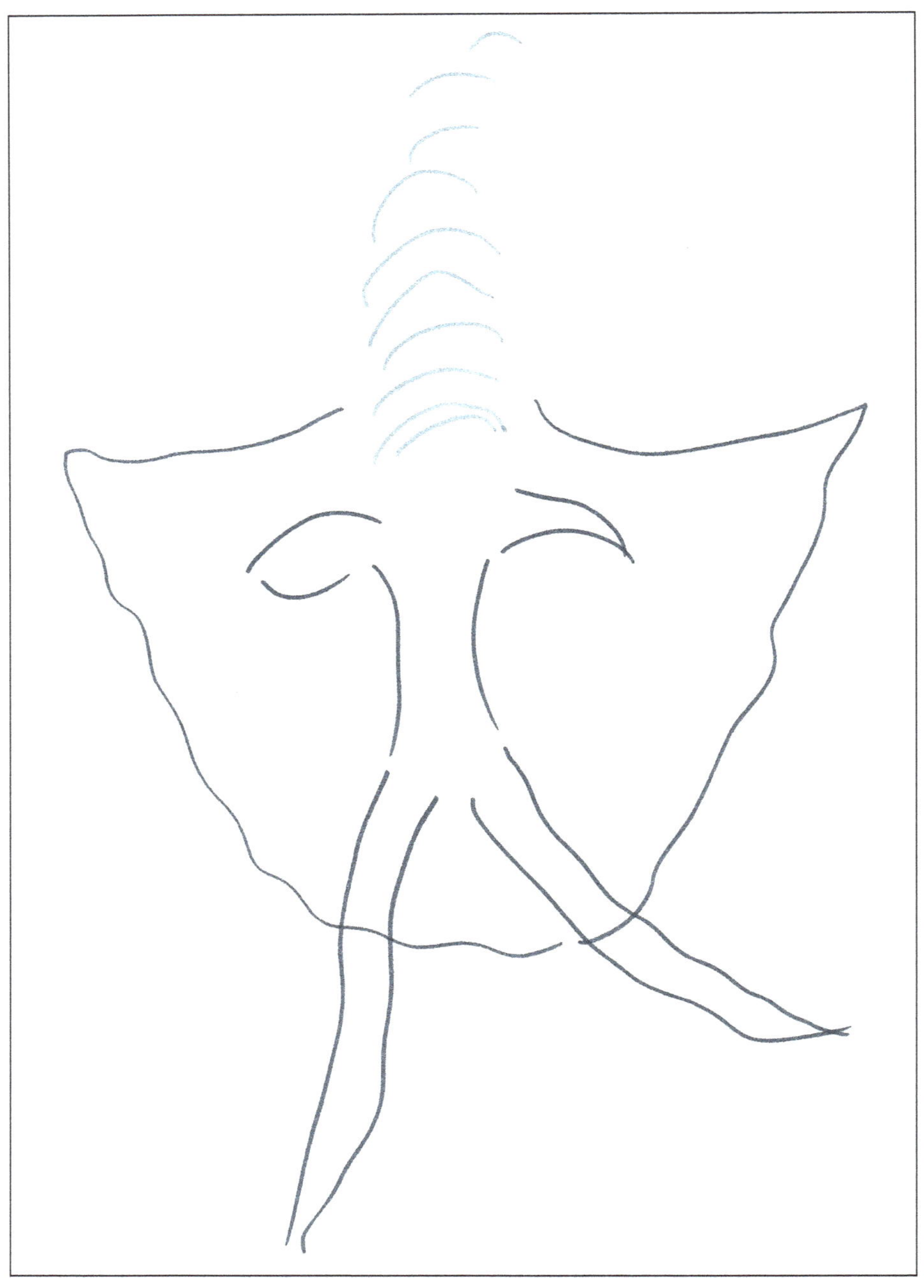

The client was thus able to make contact with her spirit-guide who gave her a message that her nursery school was soon to get off the ground.

The client then spent time in the consulting room talking to her spirit-guide as a means of giving herself some advice and encouragement. The client had thus learned how to make contact with her own special adviser whom she could consult in the future as well as in the immediate present.

The client now felt that she had found her spirit-guide, had direct access to her higher self and, of course, had discovered a new creative medium through which she could channel her doubts and fears.

Later the client reported that she had found some suitable premises for her nursery school and had signed a lease-agreement on this property. The client had, therefore, taken the first important step on the road towards getting her project off the ground.

CASE-STUDY EXAMPLE
LACK OF CONFIDENCE

This client suffered from a low opinion of herself and, consequently, an extreme lack of confidence and these troubles had brought her into the therapeutic consulting room.

The client was questioned about her childhood and the birthplace of her lack of confidence.

Because her mother had died when the client was a young child she had been adopted into a large family. The client's adoptive parents were apparently very kind to her but she felt only gratitude for them rather than love. The client, unfortunately, did not get on well with her three adoptive siblings whom she felt resented her intrusion into the family.

The client, of course, also missed her mother greatly and, as a child, had lacked the understanding about why a beloved parent had died so suddenly.

As her mother had been a single parent the client had not known her father.

The practitioner then questioned the client about a pendant necklace in the shape of a mandala symbol which she constantly wore. This item of jewellery was something which the client treasured because she had been given this necklace by her mother. The client was then invited to explore the concept of a mandala of the mind and to draw an image which represented her inner self.

The client produced an image which was mandala-shaped but irregular and contained both strong and weak colourings.

The client was then invited to interpret her mandala image as a means of accessing her inner psyche.

The client explained that the purple colouring constituted the foundation of her being which was essentially resilient and intuitive.

The turquoise colour in her mandala image was seen as the backbone of the client's true confidence but this was, in fact, masked by her inability to express this quality.

The pink part of the mandala symbol then showed the way in which the client shrank from the world.

At the heart of the client's mandala symbol, however, there was an emptiness and a feeling of unreality. The client was now invited to explore this feeling of emptiness and lack of reality.

The client then examined her feelings about her mother's death and the shock invested in the suddenness of this devastating event. The client began to shed many tears over the fact that she felt deserted and abandoned by her mother and angry that the world had been cruel to her in this respect.

The client also felt anger towards her adoptive siblings particularly because they had been unkind to her at a time when she was alone and unhappy because of her mother's death.

The client then explained that the irregularity of her mandala drawing was her way of actually accepting herself because she was not judgmental about her own abilities. The client, by this means, was able to accept that the past had taken its toll but that she should not expect herself to be as well-equipped as others in terms of confidence. By accepting her limitations in this manner the client began to realise that her untoward start in life had actually ironically strengthened her in a strange way.

The client appreciated that it was, in fact, remarkable that she had any confidence at all and, simultaneously, recognised that when letting go of the past she could move in the direction of attaining self-confidence because of her true inner strength.

The practitioner then invited the client to acknowledge that to have survived her childhood at all was an amazing feat of bravery and courage as a means of concluding her therapeutic journey and resolving her difficulties.

CASE-STUDY EXAMPLE
PUBLIC SPEAKING ANXIETY

This client sought therapeutic intervention because she frequently experienced panic attacks and generalised anxiety when engaged in public speaking.

The client stated that she was unable to control her shaking when she had to attend meetings at work.

The client, who was a human resources manager, spoke of finding difficulty in concentrating on the topic being discussed at any inter-departmental meeting when her colleagues and superiors were present.

The client also found it difficult to present her departmental report at such meetings when required to do so. Often, in fact, the client avoided this form of perceived confrontation by preparing and circulating her report in advance but, of course, this involved additional work which could easily have been avoided.

When the client had to conduct departmental staff meetings, however, she was less anxious because she was the manager of her department and did not feel particularly threatened by her staff.

The client was initially asked to depict the way in which she felt about herself at these meetings as her fear-source.

The client then produced a drawing which showed a multi-coloured butterfly.

The client explained that her butterfly, in fact, illustrated the way in which her mind could not settle on the topic in hand at her dreaded inter-departmental meetings.

The client also revealed the fact that her butterfly represented the mask which she attempted to wear at these meetings even though she felt sure that her superiors were acutely aware of her difficulties and would criticise her accordingly.

When the client was asked to investigate the root cause of her fear-source she regressed to a time when she had wet herself in the playground at school while being bullied by other children.

The client related a number of incidents in which she was mercilessly teased at school because her family was relatively poor when compared with most of the upper-class pupils at her school.

The client also felt reluctant to speak to her parents about this bullying because she felt ashamed.

The client was now invited to express and to release her feelings about her ill-treatment at school in the therapeutic context.

> *The client elected to re-enact the scene at school whereby she became the bully and could then humiliate her wrong-doers by making them all wet themselves in the playground.*
>
> *Finally the client came to realise that her ill-treatment at school was the key to the issue which surrounded her current-day public speaking anxiety. This enlightenment allowed the client to overcome her fears of speaking in front of others at meetings and to be more relaxed with her line-managers.*

WORKING WITH INNER CONFLICT

Your client will need to access her inner conflict at some point during her therapeutic voyage with you and then take steps to resolve her dilemma.

Your client might begin by portraying her symptoms in an artwork medium and then could be invited to look behind the facts. Your client, alternatively, may be able to directly access the originating cause of her disorder using some form of pictorial or written representation.

Once your client's inner conflict has been identified and accessed she can then proceed to find creative ways of resolving such distress.

ACCESSING INNER CONFLICT

When assisting your client to access her inner conflict it will be necessary for you to incorporate some form of age-regression and free association of ideas into your methodology.

Your client could accordingly be invited to examine her current-day troubles initially and then encouraged to find other occasions when she might have experienced the same thoughts and feelings in the past.

The aim behind this approach will be to identify and pinpoint the originating cause of your client's inner conflict as accurately as possible.

This approach will constitute an artistic form of free association of your client's thoughts.

Once your client has identified the originating cause of her dilemma she could then be requested to represent her cognitive and emotive responses in an appropriate artwork form.

SUGGESTED TOPICS FOR ACCESSING INNER CONFLICT

A silver thread

Breaking open a shell

Holding back and moving forward

My inner harmony and disharmony

My moods and feelings

My obstacle course

My past and future life-graph

My positive and negative conflict

My race against time

The deep blue sea

The worse day and the best day of my life

RESOLVING INNER CONFLICT

Once the originating cause of your client's inner conflict has been identified she can now be encouraged to elicit a creative means of resolving this distress.

When resolving inner conflict you can, of course, select any methodology which you feel will be appropriate in accordance with your own working preferences.

Your client could be asked to initiate some form of therapeutic re-enactment in order to settle a score. Your client might be invited to instigate some inner child methodology. Your client could also undertake some form of resolution of her own invention once her creative imagination has been stimulated.

The aim of these forms of therapeutic methodology will be to seek a permanent solution to your client's distresses in a creative manner.

SUGGESTED TOPICS FOR RESOLVING INNER CONFLICT

A black plastic bag

A bottomless pit

A burial site

A court of justice

A hot-air balloon

Exposure of my offenders on worldwide media

Hanging or burning my offenders

My therapeutic first-aid kit

The final reckoning

HYPNOTIC TEXT EXAMPLE

> ## *Exploring inner conflict*
>
> *Perhaps now would be the right moment for you to consider how you feel?*
>
> *Focus perhaps on the conflicts within your mind. There may often be many anomalies and contradictions within your soul. You can explore these now and realise that both states of mind and feeling are perfectly normal and only to be expected. We are all complex beings and such conflicts and contradictions are quite normal for all of us.*
>
> *Perhaps you can consider the many conflicts and contradictions within you now? You might feel love one minute and hatred the next towards those about you. You could feel happy one moment and sad the next. You might feel calm and relaxed and then suddenly anxious and fearful for no discernible reason. Let yourself now explore and fully experience these feelings as a means of letting them go and saying goodbye to them forever.*

Also perhaps you can consider the many roles you might play in life? You may be a parent who endeavours to behave in a certain way in front of your children. This is merely your way of caring for your children.

You may also have a different face which you show to the world. You may, for instance, be one person at work and then another when you go out to a party or socialise with your friends.

If you are the manager at work then you might feel you have to set an example to your staff. Or if you are in front of your work-superior then you will perhaps be on your best behaviour in his/her presence. In both cases you may not be showing how you really feel.

Now, however, will be the time for you to take this opportunity to show your true self and to state how you really feel about those around you.

Now will be the time when we can explore your thoughts and feelings about your inner conflict in this safe space. So just give yourself permission to be yourself and share some of your ideas in the form of a letter, a poem or a drawing, for example, in a way which will be right and unique for you.

CASE-STUDY EXAMPLE
FEELING TRAPPED

A client sought therapeutic assistance because she felt trapped in a hopeless situation in life.

The client explained that she had moved to a different location and had expected to start a new life but, in fact, discovered that she hated the house into which she had moved. The client found the neighbourhood unfriendly and her new environment was not at all what she had foreseen.

The client was duly invited to represent her problem in a suitable artwork form and she elected to write a poem which she entitled "Trapped".

Trapped

Trapped in a night which suffocates me,
The thickness of black surrounding me,
Touching me, holding me close,
Too tight, can't breathe, let me go.

Trapped in a life so wrong for me,
Pulled and pushed endlessly.

The panic is rising, the fear is here,
My heart is responding, beating hard, beating fast,
Terror takes hold of my throat, strangling me so tenderly,
Gripping my body in a blanket of dread,
Taking me over and drowning me,
Taking my breath away from me.

It's like a coffin surrounding me,
The blackness, the stifling, the nothingness,
But somethingness which creeps and grabs,
And holds me down, get up!
Get up! Get out of here!

Something shouts, pushing me up,
I cry in distress wanting to run,
The panic choking me like a hundred enemies who found
me,
There's nowhere to run though, can't get out of here.

Just let it move through you, the terror, the tears,
And wait for the sun, my only release,
The golden daylight as it taps on my window,
Pushing through the curtains to caress my hair,
To warm my face,
To stroke my emotions and bring me peace,
To calm me down like a golden angel.

> The sun my friend breaking through the dark,
> The darkness to light to save my life,
> Holding me there in its heavenly glow,
> Holding me gently and filling my calm,
> Telling me softly that I am safe from harm.
>
> The birds are singing the trees are awake,
> The sun and nature have saved me again.
>
> Dispelling the night for a little while.

This client had thus captured her feelings of being trapped in a highly unpleasant situation.

Further exploration allowed this client to recall those times in her childhood when she had felt trapped and at the mercy of her parents who had subjected her to a life of violence and emotional abuse.

The client had used her poem, therefore, as a means of accessing her feelings of being trapped which were now coming to the surface.

Investigative analysis then enabled this client to address her current-day feelings which had become a reflection of her past.

CASE-STUDY EXAMPLE
UNFULFILLED EXISTENCE

This client reported that she considered herself to be unfulfilled in life and held back from achieving her true potential.

The client ran an alternative health practice but she did not seem to have the ability to attract new clients or to maintain a busy practice.

When invited to depict her inner conflict in an artwork form the client elected to produce a series of annotated drawings.

The client's first annotated drawing displayed her feelings about attracting money.

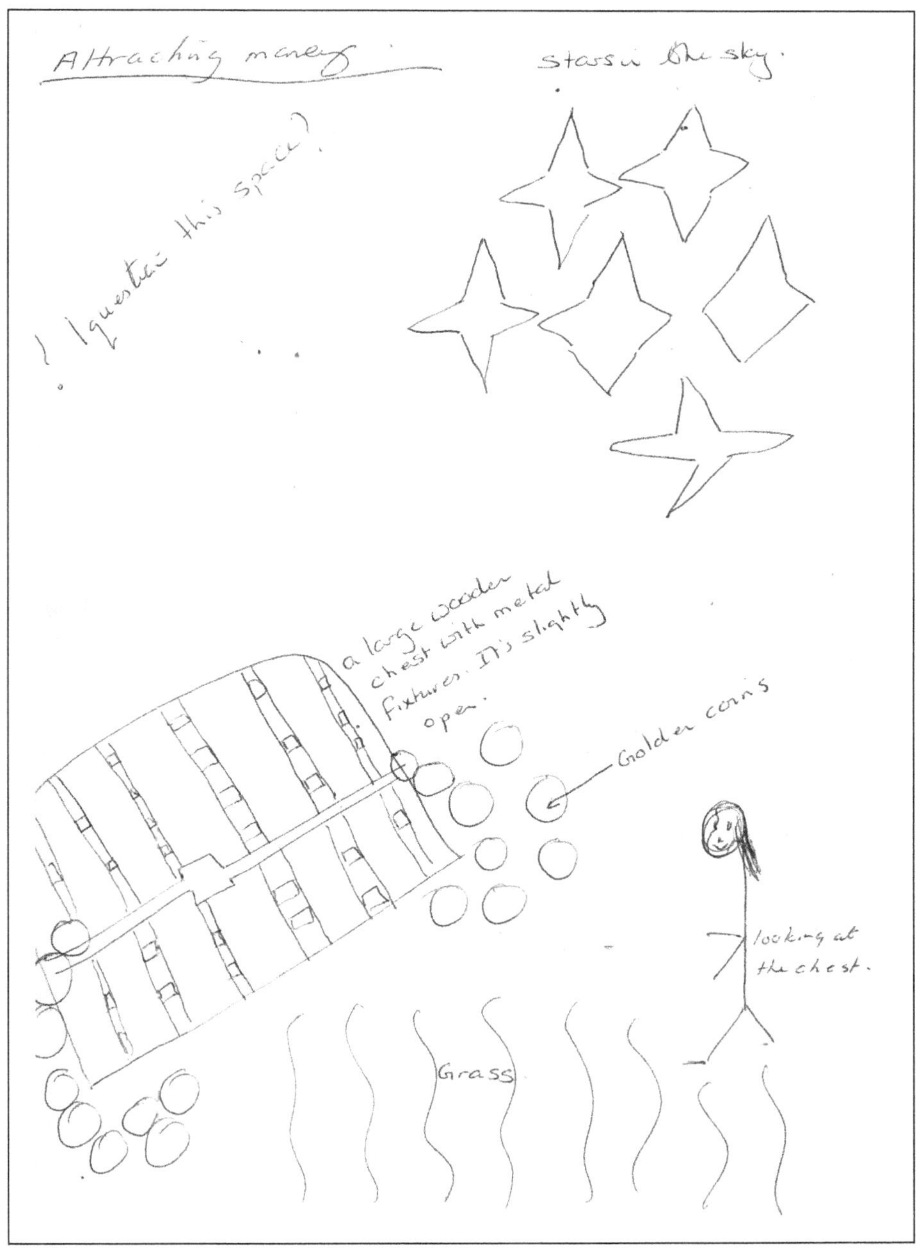
Attracting money
stars in the sky.
? I question this space?
a large wooden chest with metal fixtures. It's slightly open.
Golden coins
looking at the chest.
Grass

The client was invited to interpret her drawing on the topic of "Attracting money".

The client explained that her drawing showed some silver stars in the sky, a blank space and a treasure-chest of gold coins.

The silver stars represented the client's aspirations, the blank space depicted the opportunities for achieving her goals and the treasure-chest of gold coins represented her potential. The client, moreover, felt grounded by the grass at the foot of her picture.

Unfortunately the client only saw herself as an observer rather than as being engaged in fulfilling her true potential. The client's role as an observer, therefore, betrayed the fact that there was something holding her back.

The client was now asked why she felt held back and why she believed herself to be unable to fulfil her mission in life.

The client stated that she felt inhibited in life generally because of her mother's negative influence.

The client was requested to reconsider her lack of fulfilment in life by bringing her mother into the equation.

The client was then spontaneously prompted to depict this multi-dimensional situation in an artwork form.

The client's second annotated drawing, therefore, illustrated the fact that her mother was at the root of her inner conflict.

The client was thus able to clarify and to demonstrate the situation and the way in which she felt about this relationship conflict with her mother and the other members of her family.

She was, in this way, able to state how she felt graphically about her mother and the client, therefore, was able to connect with her underlying emotive responses which were responsible for her inhibiting dilemma.

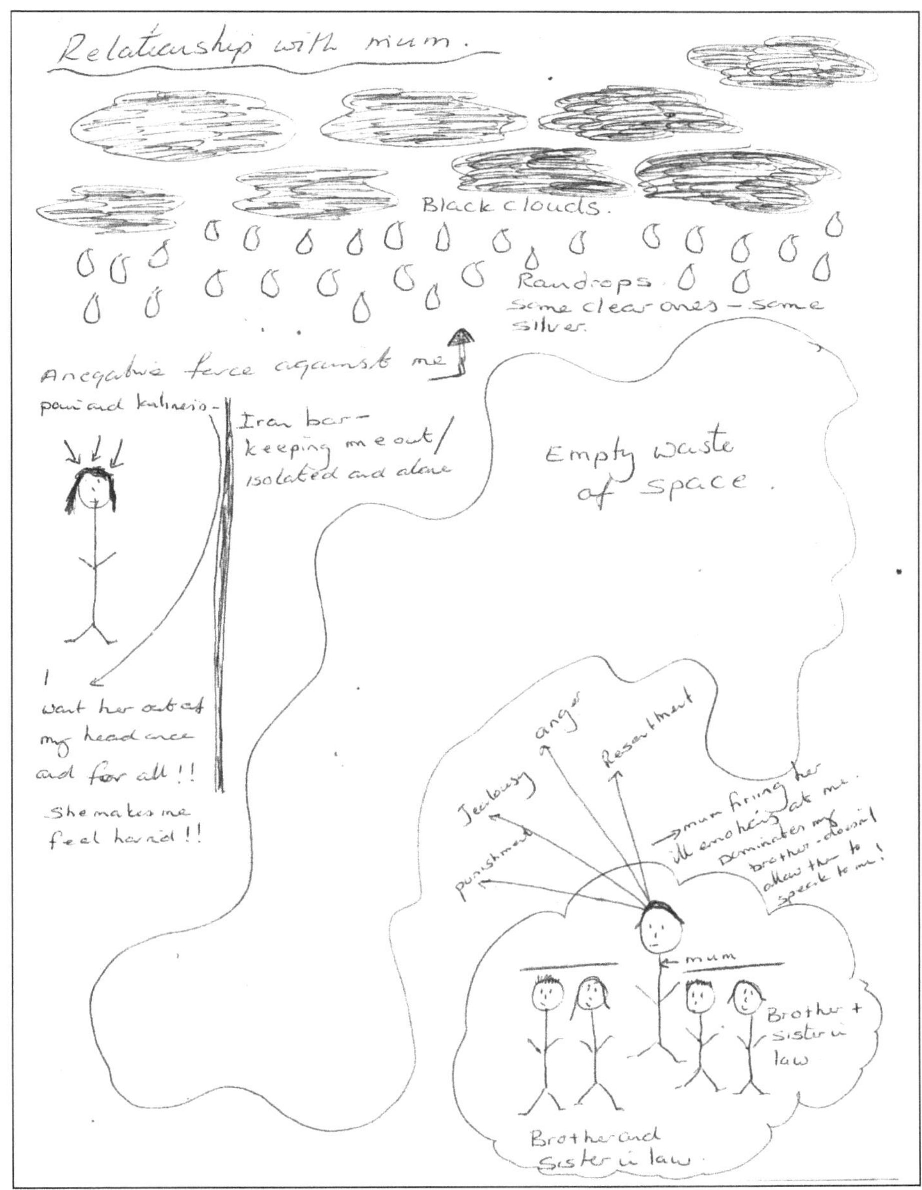

When the client was invited to interpret her second annotated drawing she spoke of the fact that her mother had cast a black cloud over her entire existence.

This black cloud, however, contained some silver raindrops and some crystal-clear raindrops which indicated that there was a light at the end of the tunnel for this client.

Because of her unhappy childhood the client naturally felt a fear about moving forward.

The client explained that her mother had always been domineering and manipulative. The client also reported that she suffered from sadness because her mother had neglected and ignored her in childhood.

Because the client had broken free from the situation, however, her mother had then turned her brother and sister-in-law against her. Now the client felt alone and isolated from her family. It was as if the client's mother held an iron bar, clearly shown in her illustration, which became a juggling instrument in order to ensure her isolation from the family.

The client stated that she wanted to stop her mother from exerting such an influence on her so that she could fill the empty space in her life with rewarding and fulfilling pursuits.

In hypnosis the client was asked to find a creative means of divorcing herself from this negative maternal influence and interference.

The client then elected to break away from her mother and to allow her childhood memories of unhappiness to fade. The client imaginatively sent her mother away on the black clouds which she had shown in her drawing and she then locked the door on the past.

The client was now invited to return to her first annotated drawing in order to discover whether she saw it in a different light. The client reported that her original drawing was now, in her mind, warm, colourful, bright and imbued with a beautiful energy for life.

The client was then encouraged to see her future before her now that she had relinquished an aspect of her past and had imaginatively resolved the conflict with her mother.

This request prompted the client to create her third illustration.

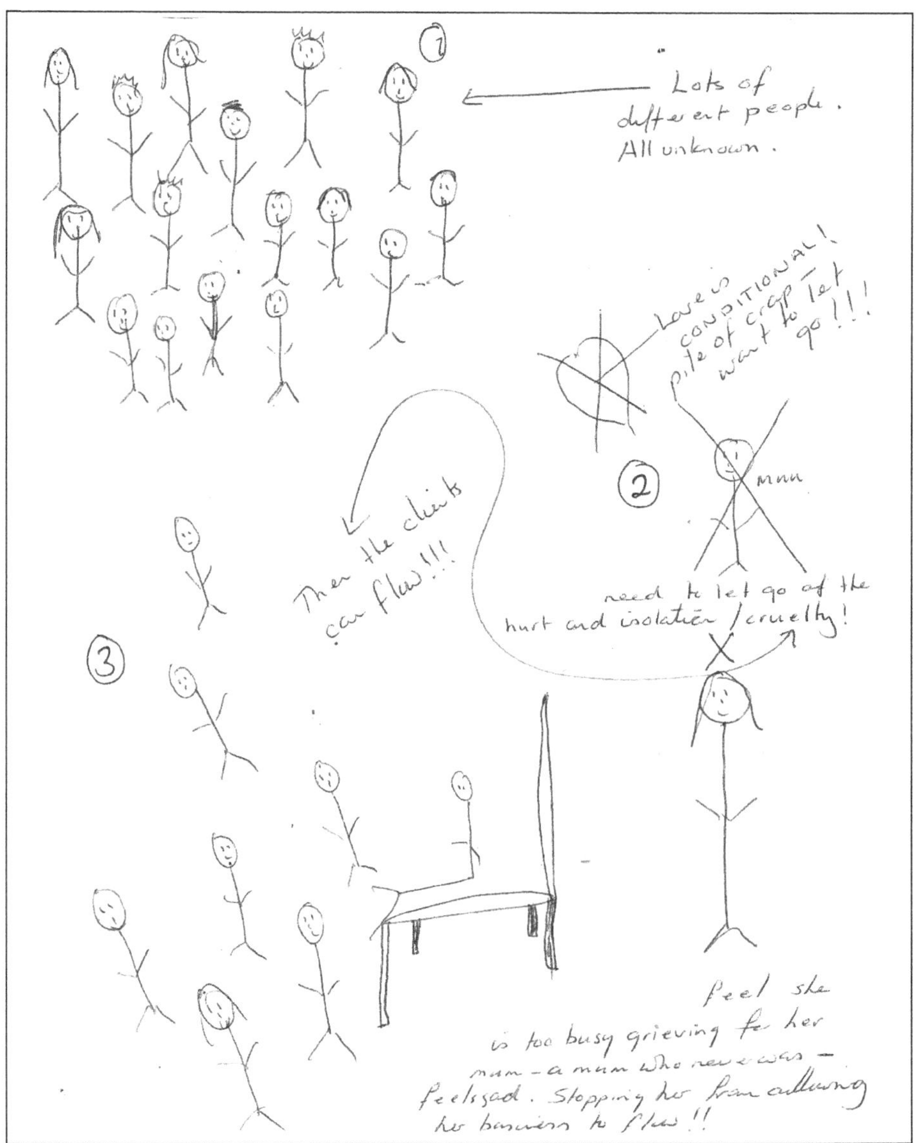

The client was now able to tell a different story about her future. The client felt that because she had let go of her feelings of sadness and distress about her mother she could now plan to forge ahead with her alternative therapy practice.

The client stated that she had, in the past, spent too much time grieving for her mother but that the time to let the past go had now finally arrived.

The client's final annotated drawing, therefore, depicted a number of clients flowing into her practice as a result of her newly acquired self-belief.

CASE-STUDY EXAMPLE
UNWANTED TROUBLES

This client reported on several forms of stress in her life which related to her children and an ex-partner.

The client's situation was examined at length in the therapeutic context. The client knew that she was making progress by looking at her own unwanted emotional baggage but still felt that others around her were a weighty responsibility and a nuisance.

When requested to express herself in a graphic form the client drew a picture of her wood-burning stove at home. The wood-burner represented comfort, security and freedom from trouble for this client.

The client was invited to find a way of capturing the comfort, security and freedom which she craved in a creative manner. The client readily agreed to find a way of achieving this for herself and, thereby, to resolve her inner conflict.

At her next session the client reported that she had undertaken some self-hypnosis in order to address her problems creatively. The client had, in fact, created a series of illustrations depicting fire and had actually burnt many of these artwork items on her wood-burning stove at home.

By undertaking her own self-hypnosis and turning her thoughts into deeds hence enabled this client to shed some of her troubles. The client decided, consequently, that she would not take on too much responsibility for family problems but would instruct those about her to take responsibility for themselves whenever possible in the future.

The client could not, however, explain the significance of the green and blue areas on her artwork but was content just to keep these colours there because the meaning behind the picture of the fire had been extremely cathartic for her.

WORKING WITH THE INNER CHILD

Your client may well wish to contact her inner child in order to protect, nurture, comfort, empower and rescue herself. The inner child, of course, will be the ideal metaphor for the conflict in your client's unconscious mind which, once accessed, can usually be resolved with ease.

Once your client has been exposed to the notion of her inner self as a child she can usually find a creative means of resolving the stressful-traumatic dilemmas which she might have experienced in her childhood.

Contacting the inner child will be your client's unique way of seeing the truth about herself which resides in her inner mind but hitherto has been blocked from conscious awareness. When your client accesses this symbolic representation of herself she will then be well on her way to depicting her distress in an appropriate artwork form with, perhaps, minimal assistance from you.

SUGGESTED TOPICS FOR CONTACTING THE INNER CHILD

A child alone

A child at the shops

A child without a father

A child without a mother

A cross and angry child

A sad and unhappy child

A scared and fearful child

An orphaned child

My children when very young

The little one inside

The tiny me

Hypnotic text example

Contacting the inner child

Often we find that there is a little part of us which needs our attention very much. It could be as if you have inside you a small person who will actually be your inner self as the little child inside.

It seems sometimes as if your tiny inner voice wants to be heard.

Perhaps your little self has been crying and needs to be comforted?

Perhaps your little child feels afraid or ashamed and he/she needs your support and understanding?

Maybe your inner child also feels cross or angry and wants a listening ear?

Perhaps the little you has never really been considered and often misunderstood?

You are the only person who can help this little one in the right way because you are the only one who can understand him/her fully. Your little one, therefore, desperately needs your help and you are the only one who can assist.

Ask yourself now what your little child feels. Perhaps you can see him/her at home, at school or at play? Or could your little child just simply be alone in his/her room and alone with his/her thoughts and feelings?

Perhaps you can remember a time when your inner child felt lonely or misunderstood?

Perhaps you might recall an occasion when the little one was confused or bewildered by life and those about him/her?

Maybe you can see your little child cowering in a corner somewhere or shivering because he/she felt cold and unloved?

There may be many places where you can find your inner child and notice what he/she is wearing, feeling, thinking and seeing surrounding him/her. Maybe he/she is alone or perhaps someone else is there? Is that someone else friendly or hostile? Is that someone else helpful and understanding or negligent and harsh?

Give your mind time to find your little self and take time to understand his/her predicament. Can you offer some advice or comfort? Can you protect and nurture your little one? Can you rescue him/her in some special way? Can you guard him/her from harm or fend off any foes?

Soon I shall be asking you to show me your little self as a way of introducing him/her to you. Perhaps when you are ready you could draw a picture of your dear little one and show the way in which he/she feels about his/her situation?

Perhaps you can now find a very creative means of protecting, nurturing and rescuing your little one and even begin a dialogue with one who desperately and earnestly needs your assistance?

CASE-STUDY EXAMPLE
FEELING DEAD INSIDE

This client suffered as a result of an abusive, violent and neglectful childhood and, consequently, felt that her life was meaningless.

When asked to produce some artwork which depicted her thoughts and feelings the client drew herself as a child.

In one half of the picture the client had portrayed herself as the happy child whom she should have been as well as a child in a coffin because she felt dead inside.

The client talked at length about the fact that her mother had been violent towards her and her father had sexually abused her.

The client spoke of the various ways in which she had attempted to avoid the violence and abuse but with only moderate success. The result of this situation was that the client withdrew from family life and had few friends. The client was also bullied at school because she had been a very keen pupil who did well in her studies.

When the client produced her drawing it made her acutely aware of the double life which she was forced to lead as a child and brought home to her the emptiness which was currently in her life. The client confessed to feeling empty and dead inside throughout her life and was angry that her happy child-self had been suppressed by her hateful parents.

When the client was able to release her anger and her regret in the consulting room she was then on the road to recovery from her untoward childhood experiences from which her unloved inner child had mercilessly suffered.

CASE-STUDY EXAMPLE
CHILDHOOD ABUSE

This client sought therapeutic intervention because she had been the victim of a paedophile-ring which her father had organised. The client had been sold for money and was haunted by her memories of this time.

The client was invited to generate some artwork as a means of expressing her thoughts and feelings and she chose to produce a poem entitled "Mind full of haze".

Mind full of haze

Sitting on the bathroom floor,

The light filtering through the white splashed door.

The house is quiet no sound is made.

He put me here when he got paid.

"Clean yourself up before she gets home",

He shouted at me and then he'd moan,

"Do you want to get caught and go to jail?

They'll call you a slut and say you fail,

They'll say it was you who wanted it,

Your mum'll be sick and have a fit".

Then he'd go, cash in hand,

From the greasy old man with the caravan.

The one he took me to, to do bad things,

A slimy smile and copper rings.

They have to touch, I hate them all,

The way they look, the way they crawl.

No protection from harm, no protection from sorrow,

Not even a chance of a better tomorrow.

No-one to save me, no-one to care,

No-one to listen to the pain I bear.

He's got his money to buy more cigars,

Beer and porn, and junk for his cars.

I pay the price but no present for me,

It is my body but no-one can see.

The things that they do, their evil ways,

It's all hidden here in my mind full of haze.

The client acknowledged that her writing depicted the time when her father would take her to be abused by paedophiles for money.

The mere act of writing her thoughts down in a hypnotic trance, however, helped this client to further unearth her repressed memories and emotive responses to these cruel events.

This client's therapeutic journey then continued to examine her feelings as a young child and to further excavate her childhood abuse using inner child rescue techniques.

CASE-STUDY EXAMPLE
EATING DISORDER

A client suffering from an over-eating disorder consulted a practitioner in order to help her to relinquish this habit. The client reported that whenever she felt pressurised by others or stressed by overwork she resorted to binge-eating.

The client decided to write a story as her means of depicting her thoughts about her condition and her tale was entitled "The lost souls".

The lost souls

There once were two little girls who lived in the woods. They were cousins, called Penny and Belinda, and they were both orphans. Penny was the elder and wisest of the two and always tried to help and protect her younger cousin.

Penny found the two girls a home in an old, deserted shack in the woods where they could build a fire in the winter and on cold summer nights. These two cousins had cooking and heating in their shack from the fire but it was often difficult to find food.

They went foraging for nuts and acorns but these were not always available. They did have a hunter friend who often brought them extra food but food was always in very short supply. The two cousins were always worried about where their next meal would come from. This meant that Penny and Belinda often felt hungry and were tired because they were so hungry. This then meant that they did not have enough energy to go out and search for food.

One winter Penny became very ill because there was not enough food and so Belinda had to go out on her own to find some. When their hunter friend heard from Belinda that Penny was sick he then went out to shoot a rabbit which he cooked for them all. Penny then recovered but she still felt very hungry and worried that she would die and leave young Belinda to fend for herself.

The client realised that her story about the two lost souls did, in fact, mirror her own childhood because she came from a poor family who were often struggling to make ends meet. The client recalled that she had always felt hungry when she was a child and that meals were meagre.

The client also felt angry that her parents had not had enough money – mainly because her father had been a gambler and was constantly keeping the family short of money.

The client was requested to imagine one of the squirrels from the woods bringing her food and telling her father off for behaving so badly and depriving the little child of food.

> *The client was hence able to see why she had a tendency to binge-ecting and was encouraged to express justifiable anger towards her parents who had failed her in childhood.*
>
> *The client eventually relinquished her desire to overeat because her mind was no longer telling her that she was hungry or that food was in short supply.*

RESOLVING ANGER AND RAGE

Your client may wish to depict her feelings of anger, rage, frustration, indignation, resentment and fury in an artwork form as a means of relinquishing such distress.

It will be important for your client to bring her anger-laden feelings to the surface in the therapeutic context rather than permitting these emotions to fester or to be directed inappropriately elsewhere.

FIGHT-RESPONSE TO STRESS-TRAUMA

When working with any form of anger, rage, fury and frustration your client will simply be exhibiting the fight-response to stressful-traumatic events in her life and gaining an understanding of the originating cause of her dilemmas.

SUGGESTED TOPICS FOR RESOLVING ANGER AND RAGE

A fireworks party

A heated argument

A kettle boiling

A rocket launch

A simmering caldron

A volcanic eruption

An explosion

Fanning the flames

Fuming with indignation

Killing my enemies

Letting off steam

Losing my temper

Hypnotic text example

Resolving anger and rage

Just give yourself permission now to feel those feelings of anger, fury, rage, indignation or frustration. You have a right to feel the way you do if you have been unfairly treated in the past.

There may have been many times in your life when you felt ill-treated and the situation was such as to evoke anger and rage within you.

Perhaps you have been unjustly criticised or punished?

Perhaps you have been misjudged by others who had no right to judge you?

Maybe you feel that you have been misused, abused or neglected?

Maybe your feelings have been ignored?

Maybe you have not been listened to or considered as you should have been?

Perhaps you have not been loved or been misunderstood?

Often when we are very little we may be at a disadvantage because we are at the mercy of the adults around us. Even though those adults might appear wiser and all-knowing, of course, they can often get it wrong and then we suffer.

But in childhood there is often no redress or retaliation for us. We are not allowed to answer back even if we know the correct answer.

We may also not be able to show our feelings of indignation, resentment and injustice.

Maybe we have been told that to stamp our foot or to have a temper-tantrum is naughty or impolite?

Maybe we have been told off when actually we were not to blame or it was someone else's fault?

Sometimes when Mum or Dad tells us off it is actually their fault and not ours.

Just let your mind wander now over those times in your life when you felt intense anger, frustration or vindictiveness.

Simply allow those feelings to come to the surface about all the injustices in your life and the times when you were not permitted to let your anger have a free rein.

Was there a time in your life, for instance, when you wanted to rebel by breaking out of your cage?

In a moment perhaps you can depict your feelings of anger in an appropriate artwork form and, at the same time, release those feelings of rage, frustration and indignation as a means of letting your fiery spirit loose?

The more you can feel your anger and then depict it in an artwork form the more you will be able to release it and so you can take the opportunity right now to do so.

CASE-STUDY EXAMPLE
FRUSTRATION AND DESPAIR

This client felt trapped by her own feelings of anger and despair because her violent ex-partner had been stalking her.

The client, moreover, had sought help and protection from various official sources because of this external threat but to no avail.

The client was asked to portray her feelings in an artwork form and to illustrate her terrible predicament.

The client in a hypnotic trance produced a drawing which showed not only the situation in which she found herself but also her feelings of being trapped, helpless and friendless.

The client interpreted her artwork image as an underground cave which, even though it had a staircase, she was unable to climb out of by herself.

The staircase image represented the client's frustration and intense anger over the situation in which she found herself.

The practitioner, however, pointed out to the client that she had, in fact, used some green colouring in her otherwise dark drawing and that this might be construed as her own light at the end of the tunnel.

After the client had spent much time in releasing her anger in the consulting room she then elected to produce another drawing which showed a different perspective on her situation.

The client now created an image which clearly illustrated the mess her life was in but, simultaneously, she had drawn herself seated upright, in command of the situation and able to remain merely an onlooker.

Using her creative imagination the client had, in fact, successfully found her own solution to her problems using the artwork medium.

CASE-STUDY EXAMPLE
RESTLESSNESS

This client spoke about how he constantly felt restless and unable to relax.

The client reported that he felt the need to be active every second of the day and often needed to multi-task because any lapse in his activity-levels brought on feelings of intolerable anguish, boredom and irritation.

The client talked at length about being unable to sit still. When the client was working, for instance, he had to listen to the radio or when he was having a meal he had to be watching the television.

The client also found reading difficult because his concentration would wander and he regarded this activity as relatively inactive.

The client, moreover, found himself frequently wanting to go out in order to bring activity into his existence, to overspend his budget and to invent new projects in order to assuage his feelings of boredom.

The client explained that this over-activity too was his means of coping with his restlessness but the tactic was mostly ineffective as far as his inner feelings were concerned.

When asked to depict his constantly busy nature the client produced a drawing which illustrated the way in which he typically spent his day.

The client confessed that he was torn between trying to read, watch television, listen to the radio and, simultaneously, to get on with his work as a self-employed architect.

The client also felt that there was really no time for having a break for a cup of coffee or a drink because his mind would not stop racing.

Once he had created his drawing the client was able to appreciate that it was his mind which was causing his dilemmas and that he needed to explore his feelings about himself and his distress.

The client was then guided towards discovering the originating cause of his feelings of restlessness and his compulsion for over-activity using age-regression techniques.

The client realised that during his teenage years he had got in with a set of friends who were intent on living the high life and he was always anxious to be accepted by this group.

The client had dabbled with drugs and become generally wild with this group of friends and he felt that his current situation was a direct hangover from this wild-living time.

When asked to explore his feelings about his teenage years further the client stated that the time reminded him of the fact that his father had died when he was very young and he and his mother were left without an income.

Because the client did not have sufficient time to mourn his father's death he felt that a chapter of his life was missing. The client then realised that his wild teenage years were a means of compensating for being unable to mourn his father's death.

The client, moreover, stated that, as a child, he had been unable to understand why his mother had been distracted and inattentive about his needs at the time of his father's death.

After these events had been fully explored by the client he was then able to release the pain of delayed bereavement and to come to terms with his loss in childhood.

The client, by this means, was able to lead a more balanced life because he had resolved his inner feelings of anger and distress which underpinned his restlessness.

CASE-STUDY EXAMPLE
BETRAYAL

This client was distressed because he had recently discovered that his partner had been unfaithful.

The client then used some self-hypnosis in order to access his emotive responses to this form of betrayal. The client counted backwards and took himself to a private room where he seated himself in an old-fashioned white rocking chair.

The client then imagined the notion of emotional and spiritual freedom and visualised a seagull, the sea and the countryside as if he were looking down from above.

Next the client saw in his mind a sort of Buddha-like figure with one eye open and one hand open.

The client also saw a silhouette of a man, who might have been himself, lying on his back as if he were looking at the Buddha-like figure. It appeared, however, as if the client were only looking on as an observer of this scene.

When the client drew the picture in his mind he realised that there were fumes or flames emanating from the prone man's solar plexus region.

Then three phrases came into the client's mind which were "Freedom from fear", "Freedom from guilt" and "Freedom from inadequacy".

The client also mentioned that he had drawn his images in black and white because that was the way in which he had seen them in his mind.

The client was now invited to examine further his notions of freedom and his emotive responses to betrayal.

RESOLVING FEAR, ANXIETY AND GUILT

Your client may wish to depict her feelings of fear, anxiety, guilt, fright, terror, panic and trepidation in an artwork form as a means of relinquishing such distress.

It will be important for your client to bring her fear-laden and guilt-laden feelings to the surface in the therapeutic context rather than permitting these emotions to manifest uncontrollably or to be directed towards herself in the form of self-punishment.

FLIGHT-RESPONSE TO STRESS-TRAUMA

When working with any form of fear, anxiety, trepidation, uncertainty and worry your client will simply be exhibiting the flight-response to stressful-traumatic events in her life and gaining an understanding of the originating cause of her dilemmas.

SUGGESTED TOPICS FOR RESOLVING FEAR, ANXIETY AND GUILT

A disaster

A frightened mouse

A nervous wreck

A quivering jelly

A rabbit in the headlights

A melting glacier

Being chased and captured

Public shame and humiliation

Escaping from danger

Escaping from my foes

Fleeing from the enemy

Hide and seek

Running for my life

HYPNOTIC TEXT EXAMPLE

Resolving fear, anxiety and guilt

Maybe you can access those feelings of fear about which you have spoken now?

Perhaps those feelings of anxiety or trepidation can bubble up from within?

Maybe you can also allow your feelings of fear, anxiety and guilt to come to the surface of your mind?

The more you can feel your feelings the more you can slowly begin to release them from your mind.

Simply permit yourself to explore those times when perhaps you were very young and the world was a big scary place.

Perhaps there were many times when you were afraid of the moods of other people?

Maybe your Mum or your Dad was in a bad mood and then you felt scared?

Perhaps others were cruel to you and you felt very frightened?

Perhaps you got told off at school and felt embarrassed or shy when the other members of the class ridiculed you?

Maybe there were many other times when you felt that you had done something wrong or had not done something you should have done and this made you feel very ashamed and guilty?

Perhaps there were times when the world of giants in which you lived as a child made you shake and tremble or just made you feel small and helpless? Was there possibly a scary monster in your room or a big bad wolf outside your door? Maybe you felt as if these terrifying giants or monsters were going to step on you and crush you?

Perhaps there were other times when you felt very small in the face of the enemy?

Simply allow those feelings of fear, anxiety, guilt and shame to come to the surface of your inner mind as your way of expelling them and setting yourself free.

Once you have acknowledged any feelings of being inadequate, faulty or just plain scared then you will be well on your way to stepping out of the traps which your mind might have set for you.

Perhaps you can take this opportunity to close any scary chapters of the past here and now?

In a moment I shall invite you to represent your feelings of fear and guilt in a suitable artwork form. So when you are ready you can simply take up your artwork materials and illustrate your thoughts as a means of talking to yourself about the way in which you felt back then in the scary past.

CASE-STUDY EXAMPLE
BEETLE PHOBIA

A client sought therapeutic sanctuary because she suffered from an extreme phobia of beetles.

After her first session the client was asked to write a free-verse poem which would show the way in which she felt about beetles.

The client subsequently wrote a poem, which she entitled "The death-watch beetle", as a homework assignment.

The death-watch beetle

He watches everything,

He is still and silent,

He preys on others,

He is a spy and a watcher ready to pounce,

He comes from nowhere,

He leaves silently,

I hate him!!

The client had, thus far, not made any reference to the death-watch beetle but had merely referred to being afraid of beetles in general. The client's mind, however, had allowed her to focus on the theme of the death-watch beetle in particular when she produced her poem because the name had attracted her.

The client's poem enabled her to express her feelings about the nightmares she had experienced as a child brought up in a children's home.

Apparently the carers in this children's home were strict and somewhat cruel in their treatment of the children who were put to bed early and instructed to go to sleep immediately.

Speaking about her terrors in her poem and her realizations surrounding this topic enabled the client to relinquish her long-held fears.

This client also elected to illustrate her phobia by drawing two pictures of the death-watch beetle.

The client's first picture was a tentative attempt and she reported that she felt feelings of extreme fear when undertaking this drawing.

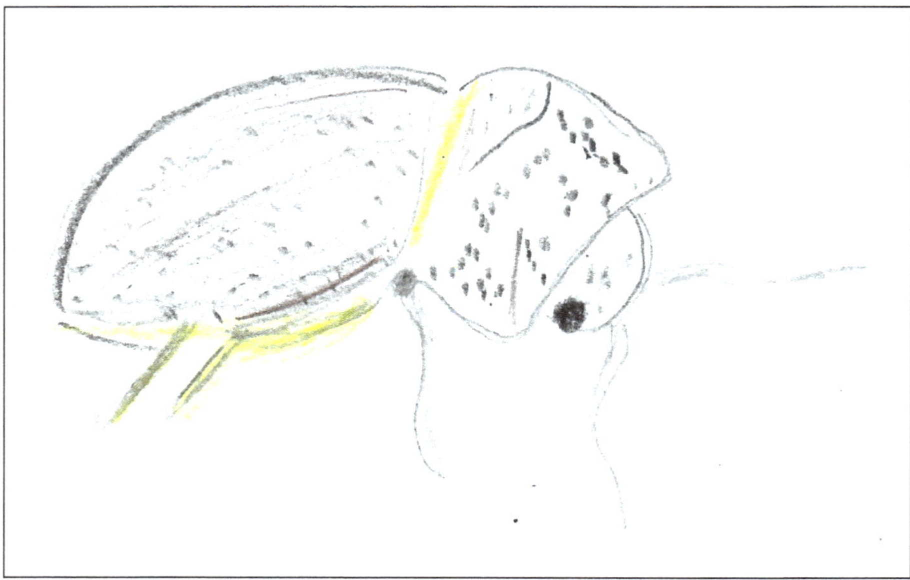

The client's second picture of a beetle, however, was bolder and more detailed than the first.

This boldness factor indicated that the client was becoming less afraid of beetles and more able to study them as an object which was far divorced from her fear-source.

The client thus had undergone a degree of aversion therapy as a result of her homework assignment undertaken away from the therapeutic environment.

The practitioner noticed, furthermore, that the client's second illustration of the death-watch beetle was indicative of the extent of the progress which she had made in the therapeutic context as a result of excavating her childhood fears about the children's home.

With a combination of poetry and drawings, therefore, the client began to come to terms with her rather sparse and uncaring childhood and the restrictions which were imposed on her by her heartless guardians.

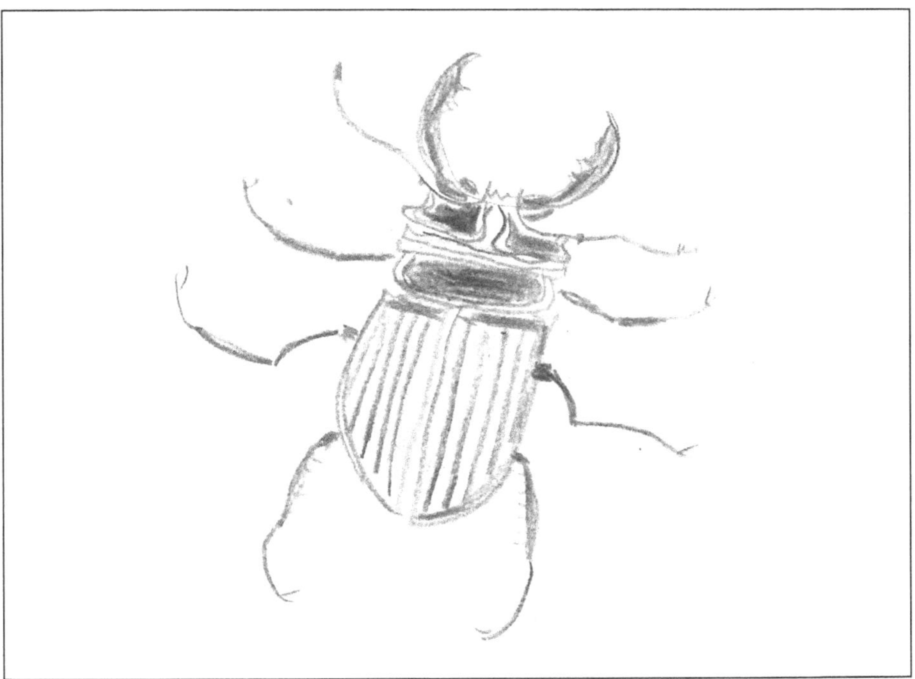

When the client's fears about the past started to subside she was then easily and naturally able to relinquish her beetle phobia.

CASE-STUDY EXAMPLE
ANXIETY AND EMBARRASSMENT

This client suffered from a range of anxieties, embarrassment and panic attacks which were crippling her life and hampering her existence.

The client reported that she experienced extreme anxiety, for instance, when she stopped her car at traffic lights, particularly those with a pedestrian crossing, because she felt that everyone was looking at her. The client also felt acute embarrassment when a pedestrian acknowledged the fact that she had stopped to allow him/her to cross the road.

The client felt similar feelings of anxiety when standing in a queue of people, say, at a bus-stop or at a shop-counter.

Her feelings of embarrassment were, of course, exacerbated because the client felt silly for reacting in this manner.

When requested to describe her feeling in an artwork form the client produced a poem which she entitled "It is so silly!".

It is so silly!

I am covered in shame.

And when I tell myself it's silly,

It just starts over again.

I dread the traffic lights,

And the zebra crossing,

That's when my head whirls,

And my mind starts tossing.

People will notice and think me a fool,

How can I tell anyone I CAN'T keep cool.

Take away this feeling,

Let me rest,

I find it intolerable.

The client was then invited to explore her feelings about appearing silly which led her to a time when she was at school.

The client had been asked to recite a poem before the class and she remembered being acutely aware of the other children staring at her. The client then forgot the words of the poem which she had learned by heart and felt really silly as a result.

When the client returned home she fled to her room and told her mother that she felt unwell.

The client's mother then insisted that she eat her supper despite the fact that she had clearly stated that she was not hungry. Her mother then said "What's the matter with you? Don't be so silly!". At this point the client burst into tears and clammed up and her mother merely walked out of the room.

The client recalled that her mother had not only been very cross with her but also had neglected to realise that she was suffering from the embarrassing incident at school. The client, therefore, had to bear the brunt of her unhappiness without gaining any comfort from her mother who, in turn, actually added to her distress.

The client was then invited to reprimand her mother for her lack of consideration, the teacher at school for instigating her embarrassment and her classmates for their callous attitude.

CASE-STUDY EXAMPLE
SELF-HARMING

This client had sought therapeutic intervention because he went through periods in his life when he had an irresistible urge to hit himself on the head and felt intent on self-destruction.

This self-harming syndrome occurred mostly when the client failed to get something right. The client, for instance, would hit himself when he made a mistake in his accounting work or with his office administration.

The client explained that he ran his own accountancy and secretarial service and that it was important that all matters relating to office administration were exemplary in order to maintain a high standard of work and to set an example to his assistants.

It seemed, therefore, as if the client had become a perfectionist in order to punish himself when he fell short of his own ideal.

The situation, however, had become so out of control that the client was fearful of doing any exacting work in the office where his office assistants might witness his tendency for self-harming.

On investigation it transpired that this client had felt unloved as a child because both his mother and his father had been too busy working in high-powered jobs to pay him any attention.

Both the client's parents had worked and he, consequently, was looked after by a series of child-minders.

Sometimes the client was sent to stay with his grandmother while his parents travelled on business but she too showed little interest in him.

The client also reported that even when he did spend time with his parents they both seemed to talk only of work and really not pay him any attention or be at all interested in his activities.

The client felt very resentful about this situation and blamed his parents and his grandmother for allowing it to continue.

The result of this unhappy predicament was that the client felt that, as a child, he had been at fault, or inadequate in some way, and, in adult life, he began to blame himself for any perceived misdemeanour.

Once the client had worked through his disappointment and his feelings of injustice, as well as relieving himself of any residual guilt, he was then able to offload his unwanted behaviour in connection with his self-harming tendency.

The client was now invited to portray his feelings of releasing shame, resentment, fear and guilt with regard to his miserable childhood in an artwork form.

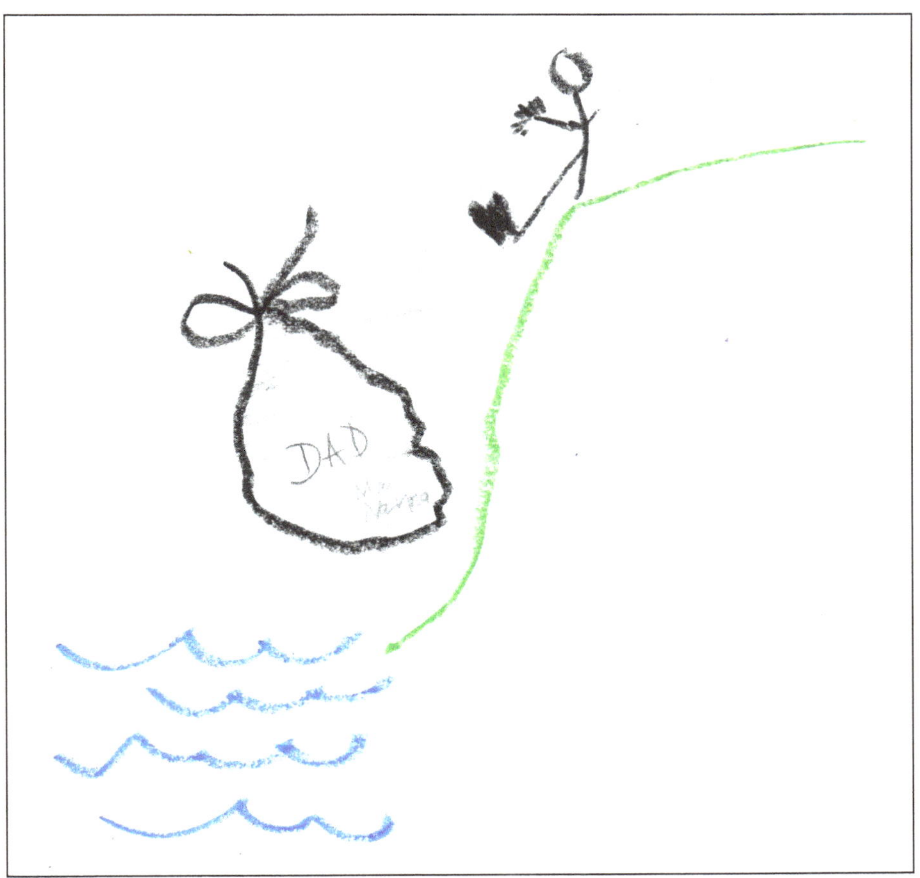

The client explained that he would put his mother, father and grandmother in a large black plastic rubbish bag and kick it over a cliff into the sea.

The client maintained also that he would carry out this task regularly if necessary and could produce more drawings as required until he was able to dump the rubbish of the past.

The client also wrote an imaginary letter to his deceased father expressing his feelings and describing his wrongs.

Dear Dad

I feel very cross with you and would point out to you the damage you have done to me by being selfish and not interested in me at all. All you ever did was go to work, eat, sleep and drink your career and care not one bit for me, your only son.

I hate you for being so distant and self-absorbed in your business matters and your customers and not loving me at all. You are a bastard! And I hate you! I think you should rot in hell but, instead, I have kicked you and Mum and Nanna over a cliff where you will die in the sea.

My Mum was just as selfish as you are and, as for my Nanna, she just seemed to go along with all your selfishness and never complained or stood up for me.

I have been hitting myself but, in fact, I should have hit you when you were alive so that you died a painful death and, wherever you are, I hope you can hear what I think about you. You selfish, cruel, unkind bastard! I hate you.

This letter then allowed the client to voice his feelings and to state his case as a means of putting the record straight and venting his anger at his parents.

RESOLVING GRIEF AND SADNESS

Your client may wish to depict her feelings of grief, sadness, loss, heartache, misery and bereavement in an artwork form as a means of relinquishing such distress.

It will be important for your client to bring her grief-laden feelings to the surface in the therapeutic context rather than permitting these emotions to manifest uncontrollably or to cause her to withdraw from the social environment.

FREEZE-RESPONSE TO STRESS-TRAUMA

When working with any form of grief, sadness, misery, unhappiness, loneliness and despondency your client will simply be exhibiting the freeze-response to stressful-traumatic events in her life and gaining an understanding of the originating cause of her dilemmas.

SUGGESTED TOPICS FOR RESOLVING GRIEF AND SADNESS

A bottomless well

A deserted place

A funeral

A lonely place

A waterfall

A weepy film

Alone in my room

An ocean of uncried tears

Caring for others

Comforting myself

Crying myself to sleep

Heartache

Tears of joy

Hypnotic text example

Resolving grief and sadness

Sometimes there will be times when you might feel very sad, unhappy and lonely in your own thoughts. We can now use this opportunity to release these feelings in this safe and nurturing environment.

Perhaps there were times in your life when you wanted to cry but were not allowed to do so?

Maybe you can imagine now crawling away into a safe place and letting those uncried tears flow?

Maybe you can reach inside yourself and acknowledge your pain and suffering?

Perhaps those feelings of being alone without a friend or a helper can now come to the fore?

Perhaps you can see yourself sitting alone somewhere at a time when you felt very unhappy and wanted to shed a tear?

Perhaps you had been scolded by Mum or Dad or any other member of your family?

Maybe you were shunned by others?

Maybe you were in need of a friend but there was no-one there to understand or to listen to you?

Perhaps your tears were those of confusion and helplessness?

Perhaps you were despairing and felt unloved in a world where everyone else was too busy to take notice of you?

Just allow those uncried tears and sorrows to float up into your mind and be ready to release them.

Often we find that there will be an ocean of uncried tears locked up inside but these tears can be easily released here and now.

When you are ready perhaps you can visualise the situation in which you find yourself and illustrate it here and now?

Simply allow your mind to show you what it needs to show you and then take up your drawing or writing materials and portray your feelings in this safe and nurturing space.

CASE-STUDY EXAMPLE
PROLONGED BEREAVEMENT

This client sought therapeutic assistance because she felt unable to recover when her husband had died and she had, thereby, entered a phase of prolonged bereavement.

The client reported that she had enjoyed an exciting life with her husband but that since his death she had felt reluctant even to go out.

When she was first bereaved the client had received much support from her family and friends but now this attention had diminished to almost nothing.

The client, therefore, had withdrawn herself from socializing and her support-network had disintegrated.

The client and her spouse had been members of a golf-club and a dining-circle but now she either did not want to venture out or she was bypassed by other wives who did not want a single woman at their dining table.

The client confessed to being tearful most of the time and she could see no possible cessation of her grief-stricken state.

The client was consequently asked to depict her unhappy feelings in an artwork form and she produced a drawing accordingly.

The client was now invited to assess her drawing and to discuss her feeling of unhappiness in the therapeutic context.

The client's drawing showed the way in which her heart was suffering.

The client then examined her feelings of being left alone without her life-partner and expressed her feelings of resentment that she should have been robbed of her happiness.

The client also acknowledged that there was a degree of resentment which she harboured towards her late husband for condemning her to such a miserable life. The client, of course, also felt guilty about stating these facts but was encouraged to express all her feelings completely.

In time the client was able to fully acknowledge the way in which she felt and this tactic enabled her to release her grief, to come to terms with her new life and, most importantly, to make new friends.

CASE-STUDY EXAMPLE
LONELINESS

This client was suffering from an overwhelming feeling of loneliness and a fear of being left alone and bereft when she might need someone in an emergency.

The client reported that she, in fact, did have many friends although she felt they would all be unable to listen to her woes and certainly not capable of understanding her predicament. The client also stated that she felt ashamed to share her troubles with others because she considered that they would be unsympathetic.

Even though she lived alone the client maintained that she would not have changed her circumstances merely in order to assuage her loneliness. It was as if the client was a natural loner despite the fact that this state engendered sadness. It transpired that the client had experienced problematic relationships throughout her life not only with intimate partners but also with friends and acquaintances.

This client was invited to explore her feelings in the form of a poem which she entitled "By the roadside".

By the roadside

Where am I now, I'd like to know?

What can I do, where can I go?

No life for me in this strange scene,

Where have I gone, where have I been?

No time for rest or relaxation.

Only room for tears and agitation.

The cars pass by without a glance.

The walkers travel but don't advance.

No-one notices my distress,

Yet I remain under much duress.

Be gone you demons, why not flee?

Will no-one listen to my plea?

I am forgotten, nurtured not,

And now my soul is left to rot.

The client had generated a poem which depicted the way in which she had felt when sitting in a park and watching others about her. The client had felt alone in the crowd as she observed other people having fun or going about their daily business.

When her feelings were analysed the client mentioned that she had experienced this degree of isolation when she was a child.

As an only child the client remembered being totally ignored by her father and frequently reprimanded by her mother for moping about the house.

The client also recalled finding difficulty in making friends at school and was certainly reluctant to invite classmates back to her house because of the hostile atmosphere there.

This form of multiple rejection had meant that the client had been depressed and unhappy for most of her life.

Once the client had worked through her feelings of loneliness which emanated from being ignored and rejected by her parents she was then able to begin building a more successful life.

Towards the end of her therapeutic journey the client reported that she had joined a social club and had found a very empathetic friend there with whom she could share her troubles when necessary.

CASE-STUDY EXAMPLE
REJECTION

This client reported that she had been the victim of incestuous childhood abuse although her memories of these events were still vague.

The client was, consequently, asked to devise some artwork on the topic of rejection and she came to her next session with a poem which she had entitled "Let me see the sun".

Let me see the sun

He comes to me so selfishly in the darkness of night,
He whispers to me to never turn on the light.

The wind outside is howling,
The rain upon the glass,
His touch is so creepy.
Please let the time pass.

He kisses my face, like I want it, but that is far from true,
He touches me where he wants to and tells me what to do,
Then soon he is gone to leave me be,
Wracked with guilt and never free.

Enchained in my silence that must be kept,
A secret I hold, the times I wept.
In the morning I come down but I'm invisible to him,
No longer needed, my life is so dim.
It cuts through my heart, his rejection of me,
When he no longer lusts for those parts he seeks.

Ignored like a nobody, as if I am dead,
But soon he'll be back when I'm in my bed.
Until then I'm nothing and no-one to him,
A little girl uncared for but fractured to the brim.

When asked to analyse her poem the client reported that she was describing the way in which she had felt when experiencing her father's sexual abuse of her.

The poem was, in fact, also describing the way in which the client had felt in her adult relationships when she had attracted intimate partners who had just used her for sex.

This poem, therefore, allowed the client to appreciate the way in which her childhood sexual abuse had been worsened because she had also been rejected by her father even after she had made the ultimate sacrifice.

The client then worked on her feelings of rejection, guilt, anger and shame with regard to her childhood violation.

The client, in this way, was able to release her emotive responses, to come to terms with her past and to appreciate the after-effects of her stressful-traumatic experiences in childhood.

Resolving dysfunctional relationships

When on her therapeutic journey your client will, almost certainly, need to explore any troublesome relationships which she might have had to endure in the past as well as any current-day relationship difficulties.

The examination of your client's dysfunctional relationships will be a multi-dimensional source of therapeutic enquiry.

Your client will need to examine both close and casual relationships which might have caused any distress or disturbance. Your client, for instance, may need to explore relationships with herself, her family and her intimate partners as well as relationships with friends, acquaintances, neighbours and colleagues.

You may find that a series of artwork items can clearly identify the protagonists in the troublesome-relationship equation and their role in your client's life.

Relationships with the self

Your client may need to examine the way in which she feels about herself from a positive or a negative standpoint.

If your client has a negative opinion of herself, displays any form of self-punishment, appears self-denigrating or seems lacking in confidence then she should be invited to examine her thoughts and feelings about herself.

Your aim should be to encourage your client towards self-love, self-nurturing, self-forgiveness and self-acceptance at all times.

FAMILY RELATIONSHIPS

Your client will need to examine any distress which she might have experienced as a result of her upbringing and to explore the relationship with her parents, guardians, grandparents and siblings as well as her extended family. This area of investigation will often be the main thrust of your client's therapeutic journey.

Your client's family relationships may be a source of ongoing conflict and distress for her particularly if she has undergone any form of stressful-traumatic experience in her childhood. Frequently the root of all your client's distresses will be seeded in her childhood family relationships. If your client has been misunderstood, ill-considered, ill-treated, neglected, violated or abused by any member of her immediate or her extended family this situation will then be a prime target for therapeutic investigation.

Your client may also need to address the knock-on effect which her untoward childhood relationships have engendered. If your client had an unhappy relationship or a non-relationship with a parent, for instance, then she will usually experience difficulties with intimate partnerships in adulthood as well as with teachers and others in loco parentis during childhood and developmental years. Both childhood and adult intimate relationships, therefore, will need to be unwound in the therapeutic context in order to allow your client to move forward in life.

INTIMATE RELATIONSHIPS

Your client may need to examine any problematic element of the relationship with her current intimate partner because a problematic partnership will usually indicate previous unhappiness in family relationships. If your client has not been provided with an adequate blueprint for intimate interaction early in life she will then be at a disadvantage when forming close relationships in adulthood.

Any unhelpful or destructive repetitive patterns in previous intimate partnerships might also need to be examined therapeutically by your client.

Your client, alternatively, may voice her unhappiness if she has been unable to acquire an intimate partner with whom she can share her life.

CASUAL RELATIONSHIPS

Often your client will report difficulties with friends, colleagues and casual acquaintances many of whom may appear on her therapeutic agenda. When your client assesses the people she might meet in everyday life and the effect which such encounters can have on her she will then be well on her way to releasing distresses which might lie at the root of her presenting disorders.

Your client may report that she finds difficulty with people whom she encounters or will be forced to interact with frequently in her daily life. Your client may, for instance, be troubled by struggles with friends, colleagues, business associates, neighbours, social contacts and other casual acquaintances. Often the conflict in such relationships will have a direct link with your client's dysfunctional family relationships.

SUGGESTED TOPICS FOR EXPLORING DYSFUNCTIONAL RELATIONSHIPS

A circus

A group of children

A man and a women

A schoolroom

Animals in a farmyard

My family unit

My imaginary friend

My personal boundaries

The characters in a play

The world of giants

HYPNOTIC TEXT EXAMPLE

Resolving dysfunctional relationships

Many people are troubled by relationships with others. From people whom we really do not much like at work or where we live to more intimate relationships with parents, siblings or life-partners.

We have spoken today about your troublesome relationship with your partner and your past unhappy intimate relationships. These relationships may have caused you much distress and heartache.

Perhaps you have had difficulties with commitment or fidelity? You may have had many quarrels and violent elements in your relationships possibly? Perhaps your needs in a relationship have not been met? Maybe your desire for a relationship to last forever has not been achieved and disillusion then sets in?

Maybe now you can reflect on your longings and yearnings for a happy partnership?

Consider the way in which you have been let down again and again perhaps?

Sometimes the loss of a relationship can seem like a bereavement for which you will need to grieve. You may also have been left alone with your interminable distress because no-one close could understand you or offer you help.

Sometimes you may feel as if you cannot make friends. Perhaps most of your friends will let you down sooner or later? Perhaps you have been very disappointed by others? Maybe you have been taken advantage of many times? Possibly people have simply used you or borrowed money from you and then not paid it back — both literally and metaphorically?

Maybe you feel justifiably used and abused by others who have been neglectful and inconsiderate?

Perhaps you have suffered from misuse at work when your colleagues or your superiors have treated you unfairly?

Maybe you have had disputes with your neighbours or had to move house because others were inconsiderate?

Maybe you have met people who have been aggressive or demanding?

Perhaps you have encountered people who have made you feel afraid or belittled you in some way?

Could someone have put you in danger or threatened you at all?

Allow your mind now to dwell on some of these issues which might have caused deep unhappiness or sorrow.

Examine some of those events in your life which have made you feel small, scared and shake with fright.

Give yourself the time and the space to consider those people who might have caused you harm or posed a huge threat.

Look at those times in your life when you got uncontrollably angry or frustrated with others and yet your voice could still not be heard.

In a moment or two your mind will clarify in order to find the starting-point for today's session.

When this occurs you can then very slowly and gently find a means of expressing your thoughts and feelings appropriately by writing or drawing.

> *Just give yourself time to generate this artwork whenever you are ready and have gained the inspiration for healing creativity.*

CASE-STUDY EXAMPLE
FINDING MYSELF

This client believed that she did not know who she actually was because of having to wear a number of hats in life as a mother, wife, sister and carer of her own parents.

The client produced an illustration, however, which depicted the way in which she saw herself free from her responsibilities and encumbrances.

When asked to analyse her illustration the client reported that she had depicted herself as a fox.

The client then stated that her fox was a cunning creature who could find a path through the woods, was quite self-sufficient and was easily able to defend himself against any attacks from other animals.

The client thus had found a means of contacting her true identity and illustrating her inherent qualities. When this client put her new-found knowledge into practice she then became more self-assertive and less easily influenced or manipulated by others who might appear demanding and dictatorial.

Subsequently this client found herself more able to insist on her own space at times when others were inclined to take advantage of her good nature. This new self-concept had a knock-on effect for the client who found a means of asking for help from others when the strain of responsibility was proving too onerous for her.

The client thus had identified a means of looking after herself instead of being a doormat for others to trample on as had been the case in the past.

The client then produced another drawing the meaning of which she could not initially comprehend. Once the client had deciphered the message from her fox she was then able to focus on her second illustration. The client, in hypnosis, was invited to interpret her second drawing as a means of gaining further enlightenment.

The client then revealed that she had represented a feather.

This feather depicted the fact that the client could gain freedom by simply floating on the wind and being carried along.

The client now believed that she would be more inclined to go with the flow and be at ease with the many difficulties in her life which could be simply brushed away.

CASE-STUDY EXAMPLE
CONFUSION

A client sought therapeutic help because she felt confused about her relationship with her mother. This client reported that she was mystified because her mother was sometimes affectionate and, at other times, angry and belligerent towards her.

The switch between her mother's opposing ego-states was usually instantaneous and often took the client unawares.

The client was, therefore, asked to depict her feelings of confusion in an artwork form.

Once the client had spontaneously represented her emotive reactions she was then asked to interpret her images.

The client stated that she sometimes felt afraid of her mother but afterwards extremely angry with her. Her drawing, therefore, represented the anger which the client felt at being deceived by her mother's fluctuating moods.

The client had also written the word "hell" in her drawing as a further means of expressing what she felt like when being attacked by her mother.

Further probing allowed the client to realise that she felt ashamed of her anger but she came to appreciate in the therapeutic environment that her mother was the person who should actually feel guilty about her actions towards her daughter.

The practitioner now had a clear idea of the client's dilemma and her underlying emotive reactions of fear, shame and anger.

This revelation enabled the client to probe further into the nature of her relationship with her mother and the practitioner was able to adjust her therapeutic strategy accordingly.

CASE-STUDY EXAMPLE
PARENTAL DISAPPROVAL

This client sought therapeutic assistance because he was in a relationship of which his parents clearly did not approve.

The client explained that he had left his wife in order to live with another man.

For the client the acknowledgement of his homosexuality was a major step forward for him and he was proud of his courage in making this life-affirming move.

The client, however, reported that his actions had unleashed a volley of fury and disapproval from both his parents and his ex-wife.

Although he was able to see his three children regularly the atmosphere in his former home when the client went to collect his children was intolerable.

The client also reported that his ex-wife had ganged up with his parents in their condemnation of his new relationship.

The client, therefore, feared that the hostility from his family and his parents would eventually turn his children against him.

The client actually felt very happy in his new relationship for the first time in his life but the barrage of verbal abuse which he received from the rest of his family was insupportable and coloured his existence with a bitter-sweet hue.

The client was, consequently, asked to depict his unfortunate predicament with his relatives and he subsequently produced a drawing of himself and those about him.

The client explained that his drawing had clearly identified who his friends and enemies actually were.

When investigating his current situation the client voiced his feelings of regret and indignation over the stance taken by his parents.

The client felt rejected and unloved by his parents because of the attitude they had adopted about his new-found bliss with his male life-partner.

Further investigation into the client's early days revealed the fact that, as far back as he could remember, his parents had always been disapproving of his actions.

The client, for instance, recalled an incident when he had achieved exceptionally high marks at school in a science examination but his parents, who were both graduates of arts subjects, had merely sneered at the subject which they regarded with contempt.

The client also recollected the fact that his parents had actually disapproved of his marriage in the first place and that the irony of their now wishing him to be reconciled with his wife was ludicrous and grossly unfair.

The client now felt free to express his anger at the injustice of his parents' bigoted and narrow-minded stance and his upset at their blatant rejection of him.

The client, in this way, was then able to come to terms with his situation and to metaphorically walk away from his hostile family. The client could now move forward in life and secure his own happiness regardless of the opinion of others.

At a later session the client reported that he had now discussed the position with his new partner at length for the first time and that they had both agreed to ignore the hostility and to go together as a united front to collect the children whom they both adored.

The client subsequently saw much less of his parents now that he could view them and their actions in a realistic light and not be prone to becoming the victim of their emotional blackmail.

The client thus came to appreciate that his parents had authored their own unhappiness which they had, in essence, brought on themselves by their narrow-minded beliefs and selfishness.

CASE-STUDY EXAMPLE
MARRIAGE BREAK-UP

This client felt that his life was in tatters when his marriage broke up and he was forced to leave his children when he left the family home.

The client reported experiencing extreme anger and grief about this unhappy situation which he explored in the therapeutic context.

It seemed as if there was an extreme outpouring of grief from this client because he was, essentially, mourning the loss of love from his life both currently and in the past.

When asked to depict the way in which he felt about his life this client elected to spend some time recording his feelings away from the consulting room after his first session.

The client's first picture represented the extreme angst which he believed was emanating from his solar plexus area.

The client reported that the act of producing his artwork was therapeutic in itself and showed the intuitive way in which his anger, frustration, bitterness and sadness were manifesting within him.

The client thus had represented his current situation and his intense abreactions as well as the unhappiness he had encountered as an unloved child.

The client was later invited to produce another picture once his therapeutic investigation was making positive headway and his second drawing became a natural partner to the first.

When his two paintings were put together the client explained that his artwork showed a clear connection between the original stress-trauma of his marriage break-up and his means of emerging from this unhappy situation after many tears.

This second drawing depicted an additional part of the client's therapeutic journey which represented the way in which his tears were having a healing effect.

The client's picture showed the angst from his solar plexus chakra dripping down into a stream of tears.

The client appreciated, however, that his grief was also bringing him much-needed enlightenment which allowed the flowers to grow again in his life.

The client then investigated many aspects of his relationship with his ex-wife, his sister and his mother all of which revealed a clear negative pattern which he was able to recognise and to address therapeutically.

The client much later met the woman who was eventually to become his second wife and they settled down happily and contently.

The client then depicted his newly married state in graphic form with a third illustration.

The client explained that while he thought he was merely drawing a flower his picture, in fact, had a hidden meaning.

The flower certainly represented the client's current state of bliss with his new wife but the hidden meaning had yet to be revealed.

When the client eventually analysed his third piece of artwork and its hidden meaning he saw it as a flower made from spermatozoa which he read as his new beginning and, possibly, the birth of children with his new wife.

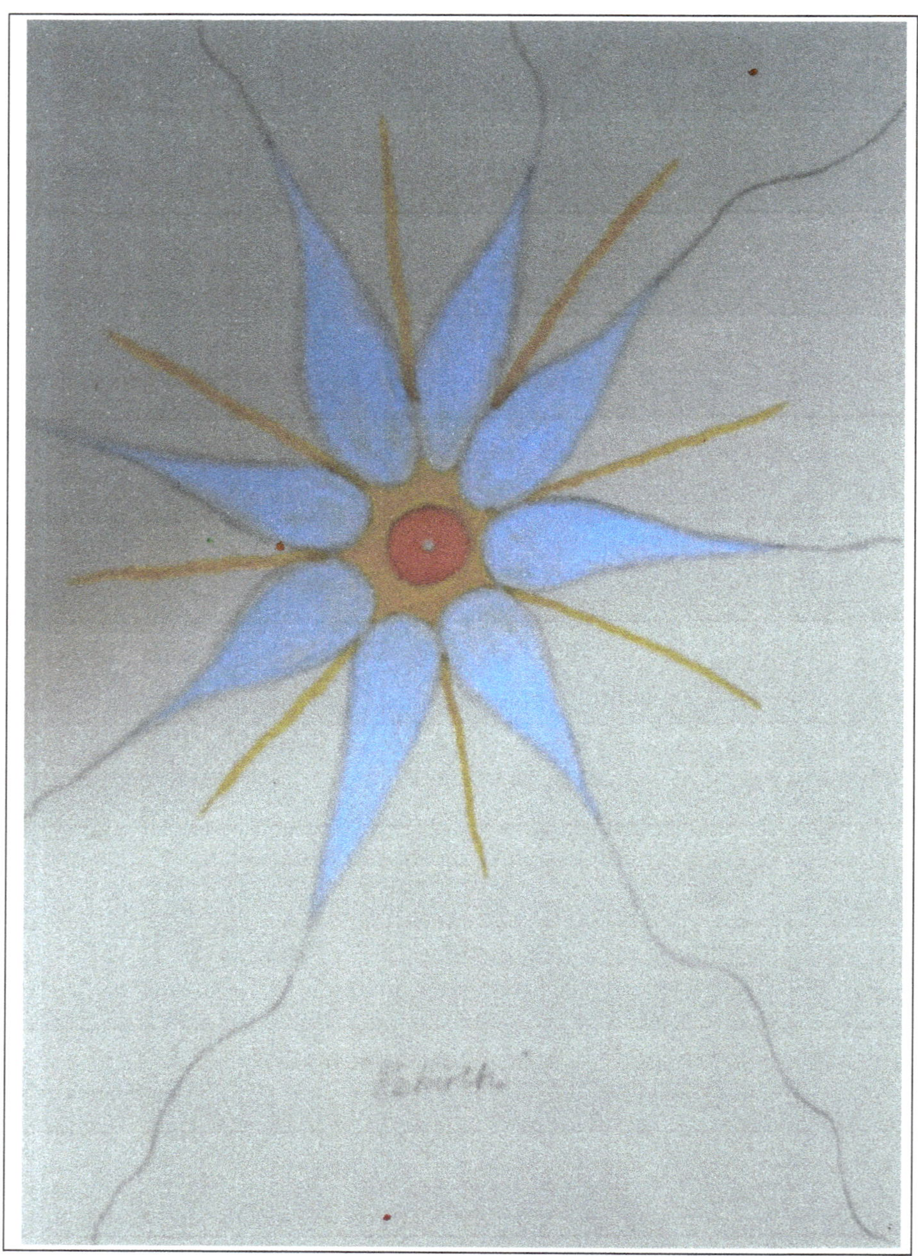

After several years the client and his second wife did, in fact, start a family. The client was then amazed that his prophetic drawing of many years back had now actually come to fruition.

CASE-STUDY EXAMPLE
FAMILY DISHARMONY

This client felt herself to be in a state of confusion and inner turmoil ard, therefore, sought therapeutic intervention.

The client reported that she believed that she was on the verge of a complete transformation in her life but that she could not readily identify its nature. The client was thus invited to portray her feelings in a graphic artwork form.

When the client depicted her feelings of confusion she found a means of illustrating what her mind felt.

The client's first drawing showed her belief in a personal transformative process from the chrysalis to a reluctant butterfly.

When asked why she saw herself as a reluctant butterfly the client stated that her family disharmony was the origin of this belief and she created a second illustration of this situation.

The client interpreted her second drawing as representative of her family showing herself, her daughter and her two grandchildren. This branch of her family was the focus of most of the client's distress because her daughter was having difficulty in coping with her children.

The client's therapeutic journey now prompted her to look at the difficulties she was currently experiencing with her daughter and the disharmony which this situation caused throughout her wider family circle.

It transpired that her daughter had become estranged from the rest of the family and that this situation put the client in a parlous position. The client, therefore, found herself endeavouring to maintain the status quo as the go-between and the peace-maker in the family circle which she found to be a heavy responsibility.

The client's therapeutic journey proceeded to investigate this situation and her pivotal role in holding up the roof and preventing herself from blossoming.

RESOLVING PSYCHOSOMATIC-PSYCHOGENIC DISORDERS

Your client may seek therapeutic assistance because she suffers from a physiological ailment which will be stress-trauma related. Frequently your client may be beset by an ailment which has a psycho-emotive foundation and this link will need to be investigated in order to ensure that she can obtain lasting relief from her symptomatic patterns.

Often a physical manifestation of stressful-traumatic experience will be recorded within your client's cellular memory particularly if her mind has been overwhelmed by adverse cumulative events and circumstances over many years. You can, however, often encourage your client to identify the birthplace of her psychosomatic-psychogenic disorder by taking a back-door path into the originating cause of her physiological malaise.

SUGGESTED TOPICS FOR RESOLVING PSYCHOSOMATIC-PSYCHOGENIC DISORDERS

A caring nurse

A ministering angel

A recovery operation

A spiritual hospital

Mind, body and spirit

My aching heart

My body's story

My healing space

My hurts, aches and pains

My mind in a whirl

My tired limbs

My upset stomach

Spiritual healing for mind and body

HYPNOTIC TEXT EXAMPLE

Resolving psychosomatic-psychogenic disorders

Take a moment now to consider the fact that your physical ailments may have a connection to the stresses and strains of your life.

Often there will be a silver thread which runs from your inner mind to the painful disorder about which we have spoken.

Simply allow your mind to view this connective link which runs from your inner mind outward towards that part of you which might be disturbed, aching, in pain or in any way upset.

Perhaps you can see that silver thread in your mind and identify that part of you to which it is connected?

Maybe you can describe the way in which that part of you feels? Perhaps you can talk to that unhappy part of you? Perhaps you can begin a dialogue with that upset part of you? Maybe you might want to give a name to that disturbance within you?

Perhaps your illness has an inherent message which needs to be received by your mind?

It could be that your unhappy self might be embodied in that sad part of you and needs to be listened to in a very special way?

Can you make contact with that unhappy you inside via your special silver thread? Can you hear the message which your ailment might be attempting to convey? Receive that message and thank your body for connecting with your mind.

Pause for a while in order to allot yourself time to discover this other part of you who may have much to tell you about you. Your mind, of course, knows everything about you which it needs to know and wants you desperately to understand.

Perhaps there will be some way in which you can communicate with your unhealthy self because in a moment I shall ask you what your unwell self has to say?

Maybe you can imagine that dialogue with your unwell self and illustrate your conversation with yourself in an artwork form?

Spend some time now in conversation with yourself and receive the messages because in a moment the time will be ripe for you to illustrate your thoughts and feelings about your unwell self.

When your mind and your body are ready, therefore, maybe you can share your thoughts and feelings with me knowing always that you are really only talking to yourself whom you are determined to heal?

CASE-STUDY EXAMPLE
PSORIASIS

A client sought therapeutic intervention because she felt at the mercy of her own emotive responses and was highly embarrassed by experiencing recurring psoriasis.

The client was accordingly invited to depict the way in which she felt about her condition.

The client produced an image of her hand showing the fact that she suffered from psoriasis which flared up particularly when she felt angry or unhappy.

When asked to interpret her drawing the client remembered that, as a child, her hand had been burned by her mother as a form of punishment. The client then spent time in accessing and discussing this issue in the consulting room.

The client was also invited to imagine punishing her mother by burning her at stake and thereby utilizing therapeutic re-enactment as a form of inner child rescue.

Finally the client was requested to depict the way in which she now felt about her childhood and her psoriasis by producing a second image.

The client then explained that the blue lines at the foot of her first image had now expanded. The client believed that this healing and soothing colour blue was thus able to grow in order to allow her psoriasis to heal itself naturally because she was generally calmer.

The client also reported that her residual anxieties and embarrassment were now diminishing to the extent that her sleeping-patterns had improved markedly and her daytime worries were put into a more manageable perspective.

CASE-STUDY EXAMPLE
ACHES AND PAINS

A client came into the therapeutic consulting room because she felt that she was beset with physical problems which were highly mystifying.

The client reported feeling various bodily aches and pains but could not account for any of these symptoms logically. The client was also, of course, in despair with regard to her lack of recovery and, indeed, questioned her ability to recover at all.

The client explained that she had been seeing a homeopath for her ailments but that she still considered that her physical malaise was not resolving in the manner in which she had hoped.

The client was, therefore, asked to illustrate her physical ailments and the way in which she felt about these seemingly insoluble problems.

The client then produced a drawing which showed the fact that her healing power-animal was being attacked.

The client explained that she felt as if someone were shooting her shamanic-healing snake so that she was prevented from recovering from her illnesses.

The client now felt somewhat panic-stricken because she believed that she had lost all hope of recovery as a result of this brutal attack.

The client was then invited to analysed her childhood stressful-traumatic experiences in order to unearth the reasons why her immune system had been significantly impaired.

It transpired that the client had experienced much violence in her childhood and had blamed herself for being severely punished.

The client was then encouraged to relieve herself of any blame whatsoever and to view the violence as cruel, unjust and undeserved. The client then began to acknowledge that her parents were psychologically disturbed but that this was no excuse whatsoever for their treatment of her.

These discoveries then helped the client to take a more positive attitude towards her healing process and to unlock her inner potential for self-healing by being kind to herself and encouraging the snake, as her healing power-reptile, to defend himself appropriately.

WORKING WITH CHILDREN AND MINORS

Hypnotic Art Therapy can be an ideal medium for working with children and minors because you can generate a dialogue with your child-client without the need for much, if any, verbal discussion.

Children and minors are always naturally creative and lack the inhibitions which some adults retain. Your client, therefore, may find artwork in any form both rewarding and stimulating. Once your client has created her artwork she might then be encouraged to explain it or simply be guided into hypnosis and then invited to review the subject-matter in her own mind.

Once the therapeutic process is underway your client can also be requested to produce a piece of artwork, or even a series of items, as a homework assignment. Your client, by this means, will usually be finding her own tools for self-discovery as a means of carrying on her therapeutic journey long after she has left your consulting room.

SUGGESTED TOPICS FOR WORKING WITH CHILDREN AND MINORS

A big brave child

A little me

A lonely little child

A lost lamb

A scared little child

A cross little child

An unhappy little child

Me and my family

Me at play

Me at school

My aunt and uncle

My brother and sister

My Mum and Dad

My pets

My toys

HYPNOTIC TEXT EXAMPLE

Working with children

Maybe you can imagine a picture in your mind which you can draw for me?

We have many coloured pencils here and some paper on which you can show me how your little you feels in any situation which you can see in your mind.

You can now produce a drawing just like you might do at school but this one will also be fun and will help you very much.

Your drawing can tell me just how you feel and show all the troubles you have had at school, at home, with your brother/sister and with your friends.

You might also want to draw a picture of your teachers at school or even a picture of your Mum or your Dad.

If you would like to take up the coloured pencils could you draw a nice picture for me now?

Perhaps you can go on an exciting journey in a special space-ship or on a magic carpet and maybe you can draw a picture of yourself and a special friend who might go with you?

If you have a pet at home, such as a favourite dog or a cat, then maybe you can show me what he/she looks like if you want to take him/her with you?

If you have an imaginary friend then this special friend might like to go with you also maybe?

You might even want to take your favourite toy with you perhaps?

Maybe you would like to draw a picture of your journey and your special helper for me now just as you did before?

When you go on your special journey you are going to find a little person who might desperately need your help.

Maybe you can visit a magic castle or find a cave down on the beach by the sea?

Perhaps you can find a little one there who might be very unhappy or very sad or feeling lonely with no-one to help him/her until you come along with your favourite pet or your special friend?

Maybe you could also find a little one who feels very cross and angry and wants to stamp his/her foot or throw some toys on the floor?

Perhaps there might also be a little one who feels very scared and frightened and also notice why he/she feels afraid?

When have you found this little one who really needs your help then maybe you can ask your little pet or your special friend to help the little one in a very special way?

Could you ask your clever pet to jump around or your special friend to wave a magic flag in order to comfort your little one who is very unhappy?

Could you ask your special helper to tell off the person who is making your little one feel cross perhaps?

Could you ask your special helper to find a way of protecting your little one by perhaps fighting off the danger?

Maybe now will be the time to thank your special helper for all the good things which he/she has done today for you?

> *Could you again make a drawing of the way in which your clever pet or your friend has helped you?*
>
> *Perhaps you can show me how your special pet or your friend helped you to feel happy or helped you not to feel cross any more or helped you to throw away your fears?*
>
> *Maybe you can draw another picture with your coloured pencils again now and show it to me?*

CASE-STUDY EXAMPLE
NEW BABY

> *This child's mother suspected that her daughter was worried about the imminent arrival of a new baby in the family.*
>
> *Apparently the child-client had shown signs of restlessness and a lack of appetite when arrangements were being made at home for the new baby.*
>
> *As far as the practitioner could ascertain the child-client had no other problems in her life which could account for her behaviour.*
>
> *The child-client was, accordingly, invited to draw a picture of her family and her life at home.*
>
> *The child-client spontaneously drew her father, mother and herself and also included a picture of the prospective new baby inside her mother's tummy.*

The child-client was then asked to see herself with her new brother or sister once the baby had arrived and to talk about her picture. The child-client then stated that she could see herself playing happily with her new sibling in the garden.

This therapeutic exercise, therefore, served to allay mother's fears about any difficulties which her daughter might have about her forthcoming sibling.

The therapeutic session also allowed the child-client to look forward to the happy event to come and to see the way in which her family was growing.

This child-client's problems with restlessness and a lack of appetite also naturally subsided in due course after her therapeutic session.

CASE-STUDY EXAMPLE
AUTISM

This young man was autistic and his parents felt that he might benefit from therapeutic intervention which would exploit his creative and artistic talents.

The young client had been ostracised at school, had not made many friends and suffered from the fact that he believed himself to be somehow different from others.

The client was invited to draw a picture of himself as a means of viewing himself objectively. The client thus produced a representation of himself as a self-portrait.

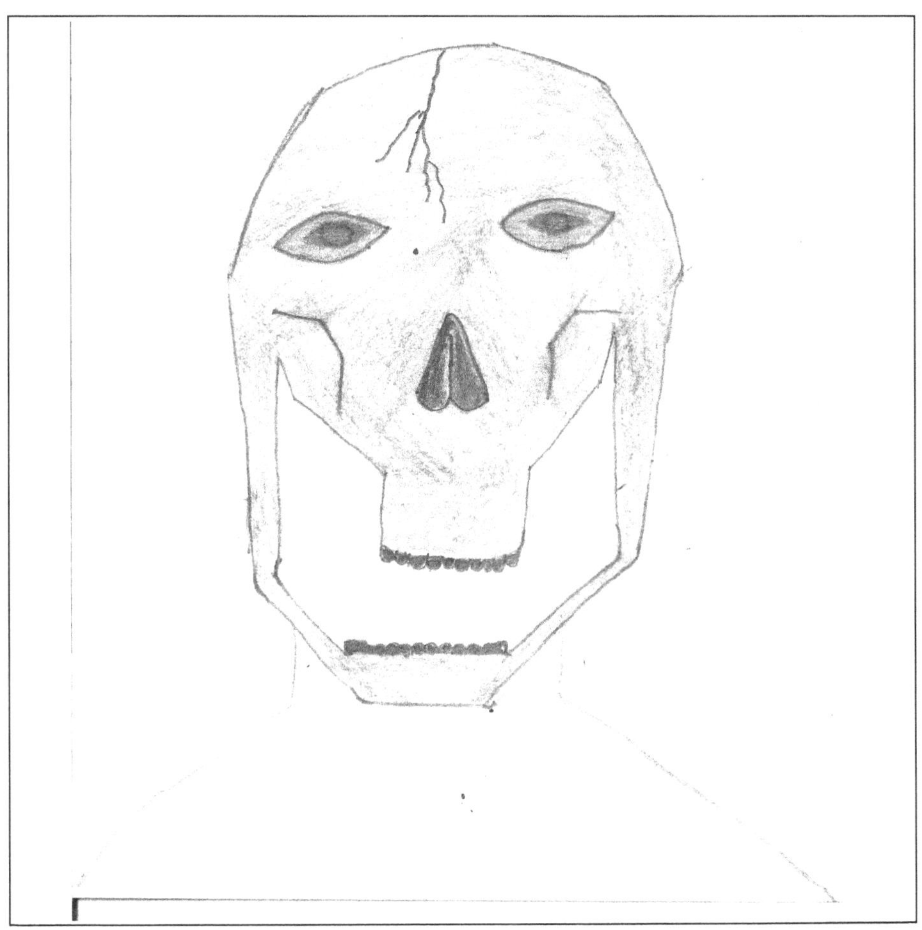

> *The young client was then questioned about his picture and it transpired that he could now see his true self emerging from the crack in his forehead. The young man was beginning, therefore, to accept himself and to become unaffected by what others might think.*
>
> *The client's mother subsequently explained that her son saw the world in black-and-white terms but, nevertheless, he had been able to identify with a part of himself with which he could now make contact.*
>
> *Later the client's mother reported that many of the young man's problems connected with school had managed to fade into the background.*

CASE-STUDY EXAMPLE
FACING THE WORLD

> *This young man was in a quandary because in his mid-teenage years he was faced with decisions about his future.*
>
> *The young client confessed to feeling completely relaxed with his friends with whom he frequently went for motorbike rides but was worried about taking a decision about his future career.*
>
> *The young client had considered training to be an accountant but was scared to take the first step and to face the outside world.*
>
> *When the client was invited to illustrate his dilemma he drew a picture of a tall man.*
>
> *When asked to describe this man the client highlighted the fact that he was an ideal man. The client regarded an ideal man as one who took responsibility, went out into the world, carved out a career for himself and enjoyed a reasonable livelihood.*
>
> *The client, however, felt that he would lose much in achieving the status of an ideal man and was terrified of losing his friends and his motorcycling hobby.*

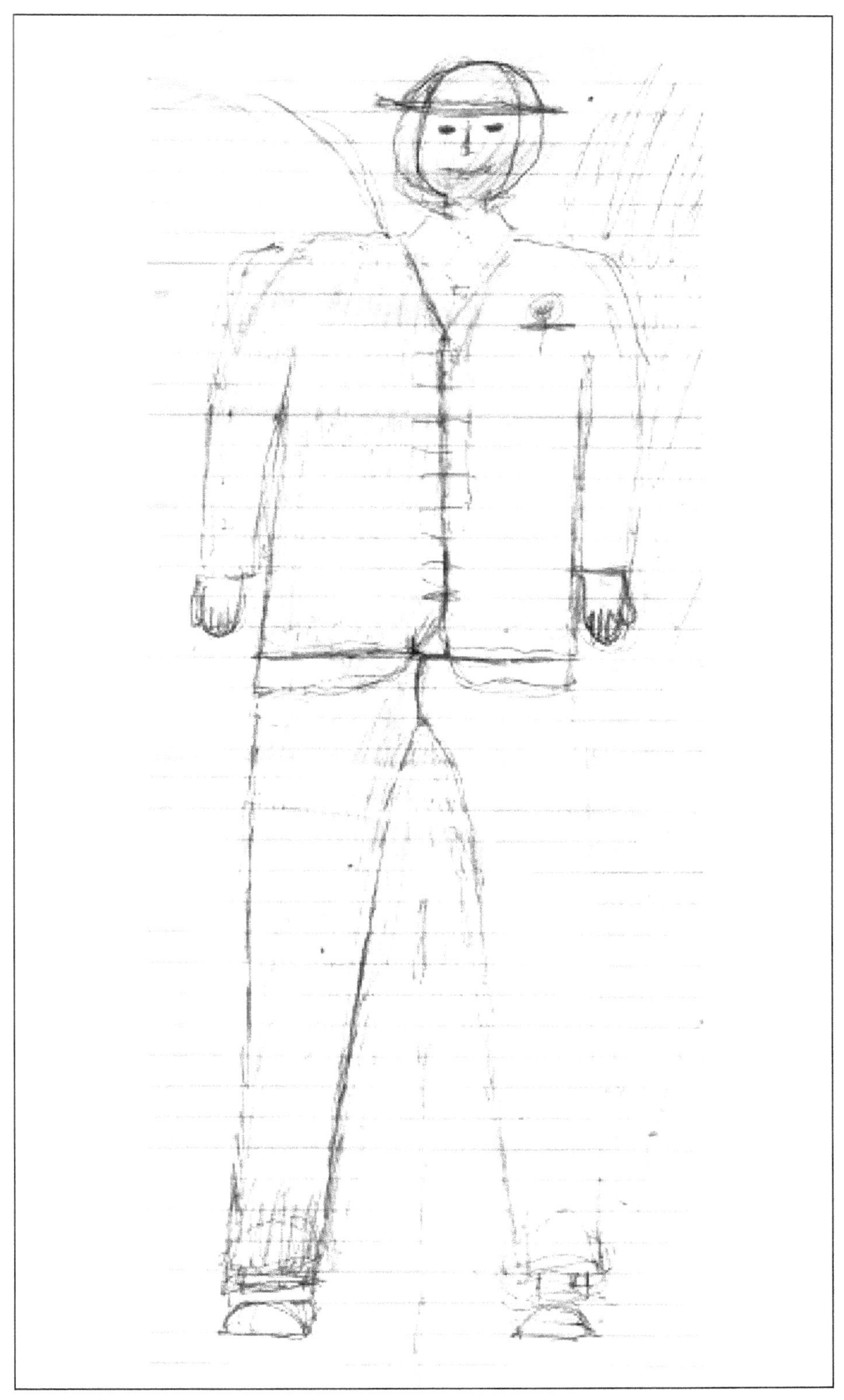

The client was, in consequence, invited to address his fears in both the past and the future.

It transpired that the client believed that he had much to live up to because he was a late child and his elder brother had already grown up and become highly successful. The client thus felt that he would let his parents down if he took the first step towards training for a future career.

This client's therapeutic interaction then proceeded by investigating those times when he had learned to believe that he might have let himself down in the eyes of his parents and his elder brother.

By revisiting the originating cause of the client's fears in the past, therefore, he was able to relinquish his apprehension of the future.

Working with Groups

Hypnotic Art Therapy lends itself very effectively to working with a group of clients so that each group-participant can benefit from open discussion and social interaction.

When working with a group of clients you can usually use a formula whereby you first question each member of the group about what she hopes to resolve during the session, guide the group-members collectively into a relaxed hypnotic state in order to create the artwork and finally invite each participant, in turn, to share her experience and interpret her work.

A number of techniques can be employed to foster co-operation between group-participants and to activate relationship dynamics in order to empower each group-member to resolve dilemmas and gain insight. Often group discussion, for instance, will be the means by which your client can gain enlightenment about herself and her dilemmas in a dynamic environment.

Suggested Group Therapeutic Strategies

A family circle can be depicted by the group

A story can be told by the group

One participant's artwork can be interpreted by another

One participant's negative motivational patterns can be depicted by the group

One participant's negative emotive responses can be depicted by the group

One participant's problematic relationships can be depicted by the group

Several participants can work on the same piece of artwork

HYPNOTIC TEXT EXAMPLE

Working with groups

Can you simply conjure up in your mind an image of the way in which you feel about yourself and your problems?

Just give yourself a moment to reflect on those issues which you feel have been troubling you the most. Allow your mind to show you what you may need to discover today.

In a moment I shall ask you to produce a drawing or to write a poem about your sorrows and misfortunes in whatever shape or form these may take.

In this piece of artwork you can depict both your feelings and your thoughts on the topic you have chosen for yourself.

Whether your dilemmas centre on troubles with others, or are merely your reaction to life itself, these notions can be portrayed in your artwork.

So I shall ask you now to represent in artwork form those ideas, thoughts, feelings, difficulties and dilemmas on your chosen topic.

Now spend some time in contemplation and deliberation of the artwork which you have produced. Maybe there will be something which you could add to your artwork or something which you would wish to clarify?

If you wish to provide a follow-up picture to the one which you have created or an additional verse to a poem then take the opportunity to do this now. Make sure that you allot yourself sufficient time in order to fully express your thoughts and feelings in your chosen artwork form.

I shall now ask each member of the group to examine and to explain the work which you have created so that we can share our experiences collectively.

Just take your time in undertaking your interpretation and know that sharing with others will simply be a means of sharing with yourself.

It will be as if your voice can merely be witnessed and supported without any judgement by those about you.

CASE-STUDY EXAMPLE
SOUL GROUPS

A Hypnotic Art Therapy session was conducted with a group of five participants on the topic of past-life regression.

The group was given a suitable induction for past-life regression and then each participant was asked to depict an image of his/her experiences as a result of the journey into the past.

The images produced were a fence surrounding a field, a funeral pyre at which some witches were being burnt at stake, a tunnel, a cow and a sceptre and orb.

All participants were then asked to place their drawings on a central table.

Each participant was also asked to place his/her image next to one other to which he/she felt it related.

The work of the group-members, in this way, was pooled and collated into two sub-groups.

The first sub-group consisted of the illustrations of the fence, the cow and the sceptre and orb.

Each participant in this sub-group was then requested to talk about and to analyse his/her illustration.

These three group-participants collectively interpreted their artwork as depicting the hardship and misery of life.

The client's drawing of a fence portrayed a peasant whose life was nothing but toil from dawn to dusk in order to eke out a poverty-stricken existence from the land.

This participant related this poverty-stricken concept to the fact that he was currently in financial difficulties and, therefore, he viewed his life as relentlessly tiring and self-punishing.

The client's image of a cow showed how in the past there had been one law for the rich and another for the poor. The poor man struggled to survive as a farm-labourer while the rich man basked in luxury as the landowner.

The participant who had depicted this image then explained that she was currently in a situation in which her partner earned all the money and provided for her and her children but, nevertheless, she was financially trapped in a loveless relationship.

Finally the client who had drawn a sceptre and orb as a symbol of royal power stated that he believed that he had been a king in a previous life but that he too had been trapped by worries, pressures and obligations from which he could not abdicate.

This participant explained that he owned a large business in his current life but that his staff were really not up to the mark which caused him extra work, frustration and apprehension about the future.

Further investigative work focused then on the financial worries of these three group-participants with problem-solving suggestions offered by all members of the group.

The second group of drawings consisted of the funeral pyre and the tunnel.

The funeral pyre showed this client being burnt at stake and the extreme horror which this tragic event had engendered.

The client spoke of being able to smell the flames, to register the cries of the other so-called witches and to hear the jeering from the spectators.

This client then reported that she had many times experienced the pain of disappointment and grief throughout her current life. The client, for instance, had lost her husband shortly after they had been married and she was still coming to terms with her bereavement even after many years.

The participant who had drawn a tunnel, however, interpreted her image as being the birth canal which signified a new life. This image portrayed the client's renewed optimism after investigating some of her fears about the past life.

The client who had drawn the funeral pyre was then encouraged to permit the burned witches to travel imaginatively through the birth canal into a new life.

Both participants in this sub-group were then asked to visualise their new life and their respective futures with renewed optimism.

CASE-STUDY EXAMPLE
HYPNOBIRTHING

A group of clients was exposed to *Hypnotic Art Therapy* as part of their hypnobirthing sessions.

The hypnobirthing group consisted of sixteen people but four members were shortly due to have their babies virtually simultaneously in the spring.

This sub-group was requested to look forward to their birthing experience and to illustrate their feelings in a suitable artwork form of their choice.

The first participant wrote and illustrated a poem, entitled "The opening of a flower", which conveyed her positive attitude towards her forthcoming birthing experience.

The opening of a flower

Dawn breaks and each flower in the garden raises its head.

The daffodil trumpets in the springtime.

The birds who have built their nests begin to herald the dawn.

The rose opens her petals and shakes off the dew.

The flower emits a fragrant scent and rejoices.

The sun welcomes all those who have awoken.

My baby is welcomed too.

I feel relaxed and ready.

I can remain calm when she arrives to the welcoming spring.

Mother nature stirs her soul for a new arrival.

A new day and a new season comes to life.

Each baby contains the essence of gold and the spirit of a rainbow.

The second group-member was looking forward to becoming a mother but confessed to still being terrified at the prospect of the birthing experience itself and was convinced that something might still go wrong.

This client, however, felt ashamed of her feelings because she had already invested a considerable amount of time and money in the hypnobirthing course which had been designed to allay her fears of childbirth.

This client was very afraid of pain even though she had been reminded on the course that childbirth is, in fact, only a very natural process and that she was quite capable of listening to her own body.

The client portrayed her thoughts and feelings about the birthing experience as a time of anxiety with two drawings on this theme.

The first illustration depicted the client a few days before the birth of her child with some fears and anxieties which she managed to keep under control.

The second drawing, however, showed the client going into full-scale panic at the very last moment when crunch-time arrived.

This client was now encouraged to access her deepest fears and she spontaneously regressed to a time in her life when, as a child, she had been taken to the dentist for the first time.

The dentist was full of smiles and welcoming but then the experience had turned out to be both frightening and painful for the client. This client had then become afraid of anything unexpected which might cause pain and, consequently, her visits to the dentist had been few and far between in her adult life.

Once the client had identified the originating cause of her fears of the unknown and released her painful emotions she then felt stronger in herself.

The client, of course, acknowledged then that worrying about her childbirth experience would probably make it worse in any case. The client also conceded that she now had knowledge of what to expect and that, therefore, her childbirth experience would not be an unknown factor. The client, moreover, was reassured that she would be in safe hands and that her midwife and birthing-partner would be there to support her.

The third participant was worried about financial matters because she was a single mother. The client was looking forward to being a new mother but was still concerned about how she might cope financially because her partner had left her shortly after she had become pregnant. It was as if these worries clouded the client's mind and made the birthing experience something to dread.

This client, however, drew a picture of the childbirth experience itself as her means of overcoming her fears about coping financially. The client was reminding herself in this illustration, therefore, that she intended to have a water-birth at home with her beloved sister and closest friend present.

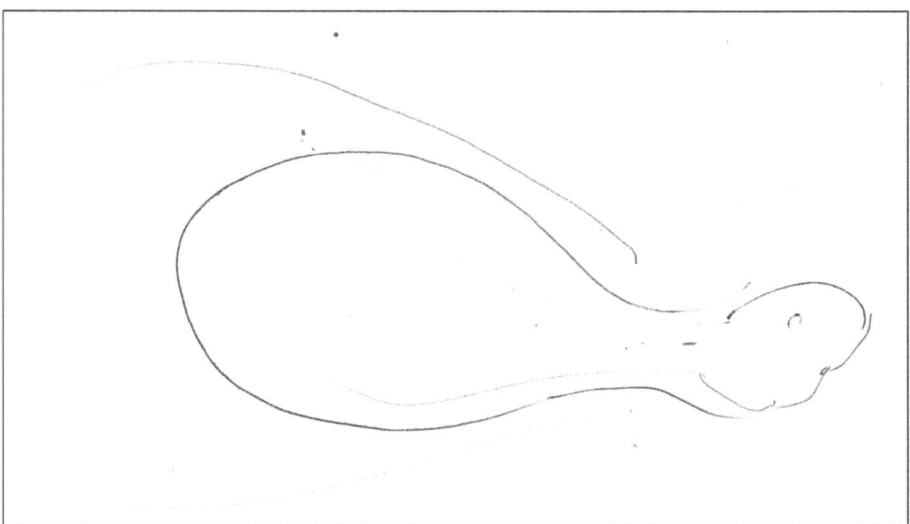

The client maintained that because she was determined to have a natural means of childbirth she would welcome the birthing experience as one of the happiest and most fulfilling events of her life.

The fourth participant wrote a story, entitled "A new lamb", which illustrated the way in which she was looking forward to the birthing experience as an occasion for celebration.

A new lamb

A lamb is due to be born today.

The daisies and buttercups in the field are awaiting his arrival. Some of the lambs who have already been born this year are eagerly looking forward to having a new friend. They want another friend to play with in the fields.

When the bleat of the new lamb is heard all the other lambs and sheep will rejoice and their voices will be heard across the valley.

The mother ewe will be delighted with her new baby and will encourage him to suckle in order to grow bigger.

This little lamb will then play with his new friends and learn how to become a big lamb. He will be safe in the knowledge that he is cherished and loved by his mother and all the other lambs in the fields. He will wake up each morning to rejoice in the new day and his new life.

This client, therefore, had proved to herself that she was fully prepared and excited about the prospect of the birthing experience.

CASE-STUDY EXAMPLE
PROMOTING SELF-LOVE

This group of clients had undergone much soul-searching in their quest for feeling loved and wanted despite having been deprived of this commodity in earlier life.

The group elected to produce a collage which would promote their ability to love themselves and each participant was asked by the practitioner to bring to the next session their items for the collage.

One participant brought some crystals, one group-member found some rose petals, herbs and flowers and another client contributed a bird's feather.

A sub-group of participants then co-operated in arranging these items in a collage which other members of the group could admire.

Each of the contributors then, in turn, reported on their experiences of collecting and arranging the collage items. All spoke of the fact that this assignment was uplifting and sacred for them.

Talking through their experiences in this way allowed each of the contributors to enhance his/her feelings of self-love and co-operation. This assignment was also for each sub-group participant a way of gaining new friends with like-minded aims and similar previous experiences of lack of love and nurturing.

The success of this assignment then stimulated other group-participants to produce a series of collages on selected topics in connection with their healing journey.

INHIBITION AND RESISTANCE

Have not often the profoundest efforts of genius been used to baffle the aspirations of the reader, to raise false hopes and false fears, and to give rise to expectations which are never to be realised? Are not promises all but made of delightful horrors, in lieu of which the writer produces nothing but most commonplace realities in his final chapter? And is there not a species of deceit in this to which the honesty of the present age should lend no countenance?

Barchester Towers
Anthony Trollope
1857

OVERCOMING INHIBITION

If your client feels reluctant or inhibited about representing his thoughts in an artwork form then you will need to deflect this hesitancy and reassure him that you are providing a judgement-free environment in your consulting room.

If your client has been heavily criticised or denigrated in childhood then he may be beset by self-consciousness and inhibition when it comes to working in any artwork medium. Your client, for instance, may have been reprimanded at school or discouraged at home when he was a child and, therefore, he may have developed a negative opinion of his creative abilities.

Your client may claim that he cannot draw or he cannot write a poem and thus cannot engage in the therapeutic process. Now will be the time for you to encourage his self-expression and, perhaps, to select an artwork topic which will empower your client to deal with this obstructive issue.

SUGGESTED TOPICS FOR OVERCOMING INHIBITION

A brave warrior

A frightened child

A play at the theatre

Fighting a wicked witch

Fighting an evil dragon

Me and the big wide world

Me at school

Me dancing and singing

My school-teacher

Shedding an unwanted skin

The cruelty of others

Winning a prize

Hypnotic text example

> ## *Overcoming inhibition*
>
> *Perhaps you can take time out now to consider why you might feel silly or stupid about producing a drawing, writing a story or composing a poem?*
>
> *Be assured that everything you do here will in no way be judged or adversely criticised.*
>
> *The aim will be for you to express yourself freely and that can only be a praiseworthy activity.*
>
> *Consider whether you were heavily criticised at school or not encouraged by your parents when you were growing up.*
>
> *Maybe you have also been reprimanded at work or by those people currently in your life who have taken it on themselves to make adverse comments? Such people are over-stepping the mark and should not be permitted to voice their remarks to you.*
>
> *Perhaps you can be invited to create a drawing or a poem, for instance, which will detail the way in which you feel about being heavily criticised by others?*
>
> *Maybe you can create a piece of artwork which will capture your feelings about the way in which others have attacked you unfairly?*
>
> *Perhaps you can illustrate the way in which you responded to those about you who might make you feel very small and insignificant?*
>
> *Now will be the time for you to put the record straight here in this judgement-free environment. Now will be your opportunity to release those inhibitions and reluctance in this safe and nurturing space.*

> *So whenever you are ready you can naturally give birth to your real self – free from reluctance and any lack of self-confidence because I shall receive your creative genius as a heartfelt expression of a gift to yourself.*

CASE-STUDY EXAMPLE
SHYNESS

A client sought Hypnotic Art Therapy as group-therapy because he suffered from shyness and embarrassment when in the company of others. The client believed, therefore, that joining a group would force him to address his issues of shyness.

The client's condition was sometimes so acute that he had difficulty even leaving his home because he dreaded meeting other people who would bring on his embarrassment and blushing.

At his first group-session this client naturally felt acute embarrassment about using an artistic medium, such as drawing or poetry-writing, but was urged by other group-members to participate in creative work in some way.

The client was reassured by the practitioner and by his fellow group-participants that he was in a non-judgemental environment which was both nurturing and supportive.

The client then elected to produce a collage which represented his reluctance to join in with either drawn or written artwork.

The client was also sceptical about the value of this therapeutic medium because he appeared initially to have no idea what his collage depicted.

The client was then invited to enter the trance state in order to allow his mind to show him what his collage represented.

The client then realised that his collage depicted his mother who had constantly scolded him during his childhood.

The client explained that the image in the collage represented his mother's mouth out of which came much venom towards him and his younger brother.

The client's mother was also very concerned with her appearance and what others thought of her. The client's mother, therefore, was overly preoccupied with the latest fashions and makeup and this notion was depicted by the buttons in his collage.

The client was requested to allow himself to see his mother in her true colours and to expel his emotive pain over his unfair treatment. The client then visualised shouting at his mother and telling her off for the way in which she had yelled at him and his brother.

The expulsion of his pent-up emotive reaction thereby allowed this client to become less inhibited about producing his artwork in the nurturing group context where other participants applauded his bravery.

The client was now able to investigate further into his relationship with his mother and the shyness which she had engendered in him.

CASE-STUDY EXAMPLE
FEAR OF EXPOSURE

This client felt inhibited by the idea of using an artwork therapeutic medium and yet she dearly wanted to express herself creatively.

Initially the client was invited to probe her fear and anxiety related to producing artwork and it transpired that she mostly feared exposure in public.

Further probing revealed that the client had been resented by her mother and yet was the apple of her father's eye.

This unhappy situation had meant that the client was afraid of making any mistakes because she had feared criticism from her mother and, simultaneously, had dreaded losing her father's favour.

The client was accordingly set a homework assignment as a means of helping her to overcome her reluctance.

By her next session the client had produced a poem, entitled "Heart's desire", which depicted her feelings of inhibition and reluctance.

Heart's desire

Parcelled up and kept safe

Cushioned by each air sac

Of translucent bubble wrap.

I am no longer content

With bouncing off the edges

Of other people's hearts.

Touch me

Trickle in

Surprise me

Tread quietly

Pierce and let me out.

In finding the courage to write her poetry the client had, in fact, found that she was naturally talented in this area and gained much pleasure from this activity.

This client was then invited to write a follow-up poem in time for her next session which illustrated her feelings about her childhood situation.

I break promises

I lived in a house of promises

They were kept

Wrapped in silk

Precious idols

Stacked

In jewel-encrusted boxes

High against the door

Glittering

Dazzling

They mesmerized me.

I left the house of promises

Ran barefoot

Smashed through the wall

Leaving shattered gems

Scattered on the floor

The skin has healed

But with each step

I press against

The shred of a promise

Embedded in me.

The client then found comfort in poetry-writing and went on to produce a series of other poems on similar themes connected with her fear of exposure.

The client in this way had found a means of accessing her own fear and anxiety as a residue of the past and had also found a creative hobby which gave her much pleasure.

OVERCOMING AVOIDANCE

If your client seems inclined to resist the process of therapeutic investigation then this will be the time for you to introduce him to the idea of overcoming his avoidance.

Your client could be invited to break down barriers or to remove impediments to his therapeutic success by creating some artwork on the theme of resistance, avoidance and self-sabotage.

You will now be in an ideal position to examine and to monitor the nature of your client's resistance and to ensure that his reluctance can be kept decidedly at bay.

SUGGESTED TOPICS FOR OVERCOMING AVOIDANCE

A crossroads

A crumbling castle

A hall of mirrors

A magic fortress

A steep mountain

An uphill struggle

Blowing up a dam

Breaking down a barrier

Climbing a tree

Digging up a road

Diving down into the sea

Exploding a mine

Finding a pearl in an oyster

Scaling a wall

The dark recesses of my mind

HYPNOTIC TEXT EXAMPLE

Overcoming avoidance

Sometimes we find that life has put many obstacles in our path and these barriers may seem insurmountable.

These obstacles to self-development should, therefore, be removed as they are of no help here in this progressive environment.

If, for example, you can see a mountain nearby which looks very difficult to climb then maybe you can find a way of scaling that mountain or find a path around the edge which is not too steep to clamber up?

If you can also see a moat which might prevent you from reaching a castle then see if you can find a drawbridge which you can let down so that you can enter your castle easily and effortlessly?

If you feel that there might be a steel barrier around you which could prevent you from looking at your inner self then maybe you can also find a way of removing this troublesome obstacle?

If there is a brick wall in your path then perhaps you can find a way of exploding it because you do not need to be hampered in this manner?

If you appear to have an iron-bar in your mind which might conceal some form of inner truth then now will be the time to banish it.

In a moment I shall ask you to depict any obstacles which might be strewn in your path in an artwork form. This will be your means of dissolving any impediments to success on your therapeutic journey and a way of allowing yourself to forge ahead in life with a forward-looking optimism.

> *Perhaps you can hold your thoughts in your mind until you discover that the time could be right for you to pick up your drawing or writing materials and to express yourself creatively?*
>
> *Just allow yourself to slowly and to gently convey your thoughts and your feelings using the materials in front of you. Take your time and when you feel really ready then begin.*

CASE-STUDY EXAMPLE
SMOKING CESSATION

This client was uncertain about undertaking Hypnotic Art Therapy in view of the fact that he believed that he would be incapable of being hypnotised.

When questioned about what he felt his chances were of relinquishing his smoking habit the client stated that he felt it would be possible to do this but only if he were susceptible to hypnosis.

Apparently the client had been told by another practitioner that he was not a good subject for hypnosis. The practitioner then explained that everyone on the planet was capable of achieving a hypnotic state even though, in any case, the hypnosis factor would not be essential for the process to work effectively.

The client was also asked about his lifestyle and, in particular, any stresses in his life which might prevent him from achieving his goal of smoking cessation.

The client reported that he viewed his life as an obstacle course which held both achievable challenges as well as failures and disappointments. The client, for instance, mentioned that he had been successful in his current business transactions, that he had run several marathons and that his family life was happy.

The client, on the other hand, spoke of the failure of his first marriage, his separation from his children and a business venture which had failed during the economic recession.

The client was then asked to portray his notion of life as an obstacle course and he illustrated his frame of mind by showing his voyage through life and the impediments which were strewn in his path.

The client was then invited to view both his successes and his failures in perspective.

When considering the client's drawing it was, of course, noted that many of his so-called obstacles were not insurmountable.

The client explained that his first marriage had been unsuccessful mainly because his ex-wife had been unfaithful and he had been unprepared to allow the affair to continue while they were still married.

The practitioner then pointed out to the client that his marriage break-up had not, therefore, really been his fault. The client agreed and also added that his former business failure had not been solely because of his inefficiency but, in essence, due to circumstances beyond his control.

The client was now encouraged to relax and was invited to consider the occasion when he first began to smoke.

The client remembered being at school when a friend offered him a cigarette behind the bicycle-sheds and he was then goaded into accepting. The client also mentioned that, as a teenager, he had felt vulnerable and uncertain about his future because, at school, he had frequently been asked what he wanted to do when he grew up but, at that time, he had no idea.

The practitioner then invited the client to review the current situation given his present circumstances. The client replied that he now had an extensive amount of life experience and that, therefore, he would not be quite so easily influenced by others.

The practitioner also asked the client whether he could now be cajoled into accepting a cigarette when considering the fact that he had achieved many things in his life during adulthood. The client conceded then that he had been vulnerable as a teenager but today had gained much strength in order to resist any unhealthy temptation.

The client was then invited to return to conscious awareness so that he could prove to himself that he was both capable of experiencing the hypnotic state and of letting go of his unwanted habit.

The client was, in fact, very surprised by the depth of trance which he had achieved and acknowledged that smoking was something which he had started as an unconfident teenager but was now inappropriate for his current life-style.

The client, by this means, was well able to relinquish his smoking habit by overcoming his initial avoidance of the therapeutic process.

CASE-STUDY EXAMPLE
CHILDHOOD VIOLENCE

This client reported that she had been regularly beaten by her father during her childhood but maintained that she was not in any way affected by these occurrences.

The client, however, had decided to seek therapeutic assistance because she suffered from generalised anxiety which was crippling her life.

The client was encouraged to relax and to investigate her feelings of anxiety but proved to be a rather non-compliant subject who claimed that she felt uncomfortable in the presence of the male practitioner.

The practitioner then silently observed that the client's avoidance tactics were possibly linked to a transference manifestation.

The practitioner accordingly invited the client to depict her feelings of reluctance to engage in the therapeutic process.

The client then generated a drawing of a tree in blossom and some flowers.

The client interpreted her drawing as depicting the peace which she felt in her life at home when doing the gardening. When in the outside world, however, the client confessed to having vastly different feelings about herself and her life because of her intense anxiety. The client's drawing, therefore, showed the opposite end of the spectrum with regard to her true feelings.

Once the client had acknowledged the fact that she was portraying the positive side of the coin she was then encouraged to look at the flip side.

The client was also invited to depict her feelings about the practitioner and so she created a second picture of the way in which she felt.

The client now realised that the practitioner reminded her of her father of whom she had been terrified in childhood.

The client also, ironically, appreciated that she had drawn her father as a deformed man beside her childhood home.

This once-resistance client, therefore, had now managed to overcome her avoidance tactics by allowing her unconscious mind to reveal her true childhood fears.

The client had thus overcome her own resistance to the therapeutic process by exposing her fears and the ultimate source of her terror in the guise of her violent father.

RESOLUTION AND VALIDATION

*The sun had recently set, and the west
heaven was hung with rosy cloud, which
seemed permanent, yet slowly changed.
To watch it was like looking at some
grand feat of stagery from a darkened
auditorium. In presence of this scene
after the other there was a natural
instinct to adjure man as the blot on an
otherwise kindly universe; till it was
remembered that all terrestrial
conditions were intermittent, and that
mankind might some night be innocently
sleeping when these quiet objects were
raging aloud.*

**Thomas Hardy
The Mayor of Casterbridge
1886**

MONITORING PROGRESS

Your client may wish to be assured that she has been making satisfactory progress but may be too embroiled in her own psychic journey to be able to see the wood for the trees.

Your client could be shown the path along which she has travelled, permitted to notice how far she has come and how much further she may need to go before she can ultimately achieve her goal. Your client, in this way, can then monitor and evaluate her own therapeutic progress.

If your client can review the benchmarks along the way she will then be empowered to continue her therapeutic journey with gusto and to congratulate herself on her achievements to date.

SUGGESTED TOPICS FOR MONITORING PROGRESS

How do I feel right now?

How far have I travelled?

Jumping a hurdle

My new mind

The long and winding road

The road ahead

The road behind

What have I achieved?

Where am I now?

Where have I come from?

Who am I now?

Winning a medal

Hypnotic text example

Monitoring progress

Let us take stock here of the progress of your achievements so far.

Take time out to notice now how far you have come and what you have achieved for yourself merely by your own efforts.

Think back to the time when you first stepped through the door. Recall the way in which you felt and the pessimism which you might have retained. Remember that time and any trepidation which you felt when starting your therapeutic journey here with me.

Perhaps you felt afraid or uncertain about what to expect?

Maybe you were pessimistic about your own ability to succeed?

Possibly you were just mystified about what it would be like to travel along this road?

Perhaps you were uncertain about what might lie in your inner mind?

Now allow yourself to move forward in time to a breakthrough-point. You have experienced several such breakthrough-points and so there will be many from which you can choose. Perhaps you would like to examine each breakthrough-point and enumerate the merits of each?

At every mountain you scaled notice how tall and insurmountable it was at the time yet how easily you managed to scale it all by yourself. Notice perhaps all those little hills which you climbed or rivers which you crossed or stormy seas which you weathered successfully?

Now will be the time to give yourself a pat on the back by way of congratulating yourself for the many things which you have accomplished against all odds.

Perhaps you can also examine any sticking-points which you still feel need to be mastered? Maybe there will be an obstacle or a stone left unturned which you would like to review now?

Possibly you may feel that there could be some unfinished business which you would like to take the opportunity to examine now? If anything comes to the surface of your mind because it might be ripe for exploration then maybe you can work further on this area?

Just allow yourself to relax still more and let your mind give you the key to what else might need to be explored. Simply take up your writing or drawing materials and let your mind show you what it needs to show you in an appropriate way. When you are ready, therefore, perhaps you could illustrate your thoughts and feelings in some way here and now just nice and slowly and gently?

CASE-STUDY EXAMPLE
OVERWORK

This client had consulted a practitioner because of the stresses and pressures which her busy professional life imposed on her. The client had worked through many issues related to maintaining abnormally high standards for herself and driving herself into the ground because she appeared to be a workaholic.

This client currently had an overload of work to which she needed to attend urgently and, after several weeks of therapeutic intervention, she felt downhearted about her progress because the external pressure was not lifting.

Accordingly the client was invited to express her feelings about her work-overload in graphic terms.

The client produce a drawing which showed her path winding through life as she currently perceived it. On either side of this blue line the client indicated the factors with which she had to contend at present.

The client, for instance, was moving house and was up to her eyes in packing-cases. The client, simultaneously, was worried about her children one of whom was in hospital and the other was out of work.

The client could still, however, see that when all these troubles had passed she would be able to behold her rainbow and, therefore, contented herself with the knowledge that her difficulties were only temporary. The client in this way was able to gauge her therapeutic progress realistically and to appreciate that time would be a great healer.

The client concluded that her therapeutic work had, in fact, enabled her to live with life's vicissitudes and to ride the wave of things which might previously have thrown her off kilter.

The client was then able to look back along the road and to see that her tendency to overwork had, in reality, shifted and that currently she was simply having to manage an excess of external pressure which would soon inevitably pass.

CASE-STUDY EXAMPLE
WEIGHT MANAGEMENT

This client was somewhat overweight and, as a result, was embarrassed about her body-image and fearful of what others thought of her.

After several sessions of investigative psychotherapy using analytical techniques, such as age-regression and past-life regression, this client was able to unearth memories of ill-treatment and violence in her childhood.

The client, therefore, became hopeful about her future because she had started to lose weight naturally and had consulted a nutritional practitioner about managing her diet.

The client was then invited to consider what progress she had made to date with a view to deciding what further steps, if any, she ought to take in order to achieve her goal.

The client then produced an illustration which displayed a new-found optimism about her therapeutic journey in the form of a magic-carpet ride.

The client interpreted her picture as one of optimism but she still believed that some additional therapeutic work needed to be undertaken before she could gain confidence and be assured that her weight loss would continue.

The client then elected to attend her therapeutic sessions fortnightly, rather than weekly, so that her progress could keep up its momentum while she was in the process of rehabilitation.

VALIDATING SUCCESS

Your client may need some indication that she has been successful on her therapeutic journey.

Often your client will be too close to her own state of mind to be able to appreciate what she has achieved and will need to be able to validate her successful therapeutic accomplishments.

You may be very well aware of how far your client has travelled but she might still need to be convinced in some way.

SUGGESTED TOPICS FOR VALIDATING SUCCESS

A big breakthrough

A new day dawns

Enlightenment

How far have I travelled?

Looking back down the road

Looking over my shoulder

My personal truth

Reviewing the past

The dawn chorus

The horizon

The sun breaking through the clouds

What have I achieved?

What have I gained?

What have I succeeded in achieving?

Where am I now?

Where have I come from?

Hypnotic text example

Validating success

You have travelled long and hard along your path here with me. You have achieved many things when travelling along the road.

You have encountered much stormy weather and many rough seas. There were several mountains to climb and rivers to cross.

Perhaps you can pause now just to look back and smile at those times when you thought all was lost but, in fact, the treasure was just round the next bend or partially hidden behind the next tree?

Maybe you can look over your shoulder at the route you took?

Maybe you can appreciate that the path was not always straight but, nevertheless, you managed to navigate the ship into harbour safely?

Perhaps you can remember with affection your efforts which were not at all in vain?

When looking back you will be able to see clearly what you have managed to achieve despite many uphill struggles.

Maybe you can rejoice now in your accomplishments? Perhaps you can swell with pride over the way in which you have progressed towards your goal?

Notice your achievement and hold up the cup or the medal which you have deservedly won?

Observe that your problems have started to break up or to disappear completely.

Notice how once you had certain tendencies but now these traits are non-existent.

Perhaps even notice those about you who are amazed at your accomplishments and the way in which you have attained your goals effortlessly?

Perhaps, therefore, you might like to illustrate where you started and where you are now as a means of validating your success and your achievements?

Maybe you could use a chosen artwork form to show yourself just how easy it has been for you to get where you are now?

When you are really ready, therefore, simply take up your artwork materials and illustrate your success with pride and pleasure and ensure that you give yourself a pat on the back for the great things which you have accomplished.

CASE-STUDY EXAMPLE
THE LIGHT AT THE END OF THE TUNNEL

This client was asked to review her therapeutic journey as a means of validating the success which she had attained once she had addressed many fundamental issues.

The client then created an illustration which demonstrated the way in which her chakra regions were becoming more balanced.

In her illustration the client also imagined the way in which her rainbow was revealing a sun shining beyond it.

The client, of course, acknowledged that she might still have some way to travel but, at least, she could see the proverbial light at the end of the tunnel.

The client took this notion as a sign that she had, in fact, made tremendous progress in resolving her troubles and she could now forge ahead to experience new things and to enjoy a contented life.

The client then felt confident enough to take a break from her therapeutic sessions and to rehabilitate herself into her new life.

The practitioner later learned that this client had found a different job and was starting a completely new career as evidence of her new-found freedom and happiness.

CASE-STUDY EXAMPLE
RAPE VICTIM

This client sought therapeutic help because she had been raped in her teenage years by a casual acquaintance and then was forced to have a pregnancy termination because she had become pregnant during the attack.

This rape incident then led the client to fail most of her school examinations and, to make matters worse, she was not treated very sympathetically by her teachers despite the fact that the school had been informed of her tragedy.

The client then had to find employment without any appropriate qualifications and, in consequence, was compelled to accept menial work which did not match her intelligence-level.

The client had thus developed a sense of low self-worth and a poor self-image as a result of the date-rape during her teenage years and its consequent after-effects.

The client discussed the rape incident at length with the practitioner who used a combination of age-regression, therapeutic re-enactment, inner child work and inner adviser methodology in order to assist her to release her feelings of resentment, shame, guilt and shock.

Throughout her therapeutic encounter the client had written a series of poems in order to portray her deepest feelings.

Towards the end of her therapeutic journey the client was, therefore, requested to consider her current position as a means of validating her therapeutic success.

The client accordingly wrote a poem, entitled "Change", which clearly validated her therapeutic success.

Change

And when the time is right for you,

You'll find you want to change it too.

No more crying on the stairs,

Asking a god to answer prayers.

Make your map and follow your path,

Be at peace and learn to laugh.

Open your heart and make a space,

You'll find the world a beautiful place.

Beliefs are real and deep inside,

Some you feel you want to hide.

But they always rise to let you see,

There's something there you need not be.

The client's poem thus clearly demonstrated the way in which her therapeutic quest had progressed to such a point that her success was tangible and could be truly validated.

EXPANDING HORIZONS

Often your client will be concerned with looking inwardly as a means of overcoming her difficulties in the therapeutic context. Towards the end of her therapeutic journey with you, therefore, your client could be encouraged to expand her horizons as a way of thinking more openly about the future.

Your client could be encouraged to tackle her life with renewed optimism and strength. Your client could also be invited to lead a much healthier life and to fulfil her potential in terms of her life's work or her personal mission. Your client could, moreover, empower herself by taking an optimistic view of any unknown challenges with which she might yet be faced in the future.

Often your client will have to come to terms with living with uncertainty along life's path and her therapeutic journey will be the ideal medium for embracing this uncertainty.

SUGGESTED TOPICS FOR EXPANDING HORIZONS

A magic cave

A message in the clouds

A mountain and a molehill

An enchanted den

Grant me a wish

Inside and outside the box

My future aspirations

Overcoming my future challenges

Planting a seed and watching it grow

The fairies at the bottom of the garden

HYPNOTIC TEXT EXAMPLE

Expanding horizons

Permit your mind to open up in a way which you might never have thought possible before.

Make a note in your mind to allow your horizons to expand naturally.

Perhaps you can allow your perspective to expand as it would naturally if you were standing on a beach and looking far out to sea? Maybe you can see a ship on the horizon which might be bringing you a special treasure? Perhaps when excitedly opening that treasure-chest you can realise that it is well deserved by you and will be there in abundance for your own pleasure?

Perhaps you can visualise yourself at the top of a mountain looking down into a vast valley or across the mountain-tops far in the distance? Maybe you can see the flowers which grow at the top of your mountain and appreciate that these blossoms have grown for you alone to receive as a gift?

You might even see yourself walking on a flat plain where you can see for miles and miles with a 360-degree view of the landscape. Here you might wish to capture some of the vastness and the majesty of nature as a means of making it your own. Maybe you can harness some of that awesome power by taking it into your soul and claiming it as your own?

Imagine sitting at the top of your world having won the race of all time and gaining a prize which is second to none. This will be your reward many years after you have left this place and forgotten my existence. Let yourself claim this much-deserved prize as a means of expanding your horizons in the future.

Perhaps your image of this personal expansion can be recorded by you in an appropriate artwork form? Maybe, therefore, you can depict your thoughts and feelings about expanding your horizons, your life and your future with your new-found enlightenment?

So when you are ready to show me and yourself what you have been visualizing then simply take up your drawing or writing materials and express yourself freely in the most appropriate way.

CASE-STUDY EXAMPLE
DOMESTIC VIOLENCE

This client came for therapeutic assistance because his anger had resulted in violence towards his partner who had promptly deserted him.

The client was highly distressed at this partnership break-up but appreciated that his ex-partner would obviously not now return to him as a direct result of his violent tendencies. The client, however, wanted desperately to overcome his uncontrollable violence and to find another woman with whom he could share his life.

The client then began to investigate his childhood in which his father had beaten him and his parents had been violent towards each other. Therapeutic investigation, consequently, allowed this client to realise that his current-day violent tendencies had been seeded way back in his childhood when he had been not only the recipient of violence but also surrounded by unbridled aggression.

After several sessions in which the client had expressed his anger in the appropriate direction he reported that his inclination to uncontrollable outbursts of anger had begun to subside. The client stated that he no longer wished, for example, to shout at other motorists or to throw chairs across the room when he was in an angry mood.

The client was, therefore, led to realise that once his childhood difficulties were acknowledged and fully expressed he could then begin to rebuild his life.

The client now elected to depict the uphill struggle he had experienced from early childhood onwards.

From his drawing the client could now appreciate that his courage in addressing his painful issues would virtually guarantee a brighter future.

The client also realised that his former partner had exhibited a tendency to severely criticise him and to belittle him in front of others and was, therefore, fundamentally unsuitable for him now as a long-term partner.

CASE-STUDY EXAMPLE
FEAR OF FLYING

This client had worked for some time on her fear of flying and had undergone her first trouble-free flight.

The client reported that she had not felt compelled to resort to alcohol in order to even board the plane and had not had a panic attack in mid-air.

The client, however, still felt that the experience had held some trepidation for her and was nervous about making another attempt to fly particularly if the flight were to experience turbulence.

The client's fear of flying had been largely the result of her mother's anxieties. In her early childhood the client had travelled on a plane with her mother who had, for the first time, manifested her fear and anxiety.

The client, who felt that her mother was normally the strong and reliable support in her life, suddenly realised that her mother was, in fact, highly vulnerable.

This knowledge profoundly affected the client whose own anxieties, in turn, manifested when she boarded a plane in her teenage years in order to go on holiday. The client then found herself unable to make the return journey by plane and had to return overland instead.

Further exploration into the notions of insecurity, feeling vulnerable and abandoned were undertaken by the client who then felt herself to be stronger. The client was accordingly asked to depict her change of heart and to portray her prospect of flying in the future.

The client then produced a drawing which showed a rainbow.

The client explained that she now felt much happier about the prospect of flying in future and actually looked forward to the event.

The client appreciated that her fear of flying, moreover, was a blanket term for her doubt, insecurities and anxieties which had dogged her for most of her life but which were now beginning to pale into insignificance.

EMBRACING THE FUTURE

At the end of your client's therapeutic journey with you she may wish to look to the future. Your client might be keen, for example, to visualise her road ahead in terms of her emotive reactions and her symptomatic patterns.

When seeking to embrace the future your client may also be providing herself with evidence of her therapeutic progress and success as well as looking ahead to the time when she will be free in any situation in which she might previously have felt vulnerable. Your client, for instance, could see herself without her fears and a panic-stricken response. Your client might also regard herself without the need to resort to over-indulgence or excessive self-punishment. Your client might, furthermore, regard herself as being free from a negative feeling when she encounters someone who, in the past, might have triggered her distress.

SUGGESTED TOPICS FOR EMBRACING THE FUTURE

A crystal ball

A mode of transport into the future

A path out of the woods

A self-nurturing personal gift

An uncertain future

Change and stability

Looking ahead

Seeing what might be in store for me

Temptation and vulnerability

The beginning and the end of a journey

The road ahead

Hypnotic text example

Embracing the future

Soon the time will arrive for you to leave the therapeutic environment in order to enjoy a happy future.

Now that you have excavated the past it will be time for you to consider your future life away from this therapeutic enclave. Maybe you can imagine yourself enjoying life in a different way? Maybe you can look at yourself as you might be in three months' time or in six months' time? Possibly you might want to look ahead to next year or to the next five years or even further into the future?

See yourself, for instance, in a different world. Notice the way in which you can embrace the future and can live in an uncertain world with confidence. Maybe you can see yourself with better habits or leading a healthier existence? Perhaps you can envisage the way in which you will be fulfilling your potential in years to come? Maybe your dreams will be realised sooner rather than later?

Now you can embark on that voyage of discovery having left behind those things which held you back in life in the past. The future will be an exciting place now that you are leaving the past behind you. Perhaps, in your mind, you can open your arms in order to embrace a bright and happy future free from worries and troubles? Maybe see yourself well able to encounter any obstacles or impediments which might have, in the past, thrown you off course?

You will now be easily able to deal with anything untoward which may arise with ease, conviction and confidence. It will be as if you can take anything in your stride and still keep the ship afloat single-handedly. Know now that you will win the race with absolute certainty.

Finally allow yourself to depict your newly discovered optimism by taking up your drawing or writing materials and illustrating what life will be like for you in the future.

Perhaps show how confident and capable you have become or indicate a straight path ahead of you?

Maybe you can view your guiding star with much abundance and assistance along the way?

So, when you are ready, now will be the time to begin your new life in your own special way.

CASE-STUDY EXAMPLE
REBIRTHING

This client had worked extensively on improving her self-concept and now wanted to gauge how she actually felt about herself.

First the client depicted herself as if she were metaphorically all at sea.

The client explained in hypnosis that she was floating on the waves and feeling at the mercy of the elements.

The client was then invited to interpret her feelings and she spoke about how she had been pushed from pillar to post by teachers at school and colleagues at work for many years. The client also cited a number of instances when she had been ill-used unfairly by others particularly within intimate relationships.

The client was then encouraged to allow her feelings of frustration and injustice to float to the bottom of the sea.

Next the client was invited to allow those people in her life who had treated her unfairly or unjustly to be left at the bottom of the sea wearing lead boots.

The client then depicted her new-found psyche in a very different guise.

The drawing which the client created now showed her sitting on the grass. The picture represented the client in a relaxed mood and with an upright back.

The client explained that she was sitting proudly and looking on the world with purpose and determination having left her former feelings of debased self-esteem behind her.

The client now, in concluding her therapeutic quest, believed that she was ready to face the future as if she had been reborn.

CASE-STUDY EXAMPLE
UNCERTAIN FUTURE

This client had been undecided about whether or not to stay with his wife and had sought therapeutic assistance in order to explore his feelings and to take a decision.

The client reported that he had been contemplating leaving his wife but was concerned for his two children and the distress which such a family upheaval would cause them.

In the therapeutic context the client then examined his relationship with his wife and concluded finally that the relationship was irretrievably dead and had been so for many years.

The client acknowledged, moreover, that his children were, in fact, suffering by his remaining in this fruitless and destructive relationship.

For these reasons the client elected to leave his wife and his dilemma was, therefore, resolved.

It was hence time for the client to face the future now that he had taken his decision to depart from the family home.

When asked to view his future the client produced a drawing of a crystal ball.

The client explained that once he had jumped the hurdle of telling his wife that he was moving out he would be faced with an uncertain future.

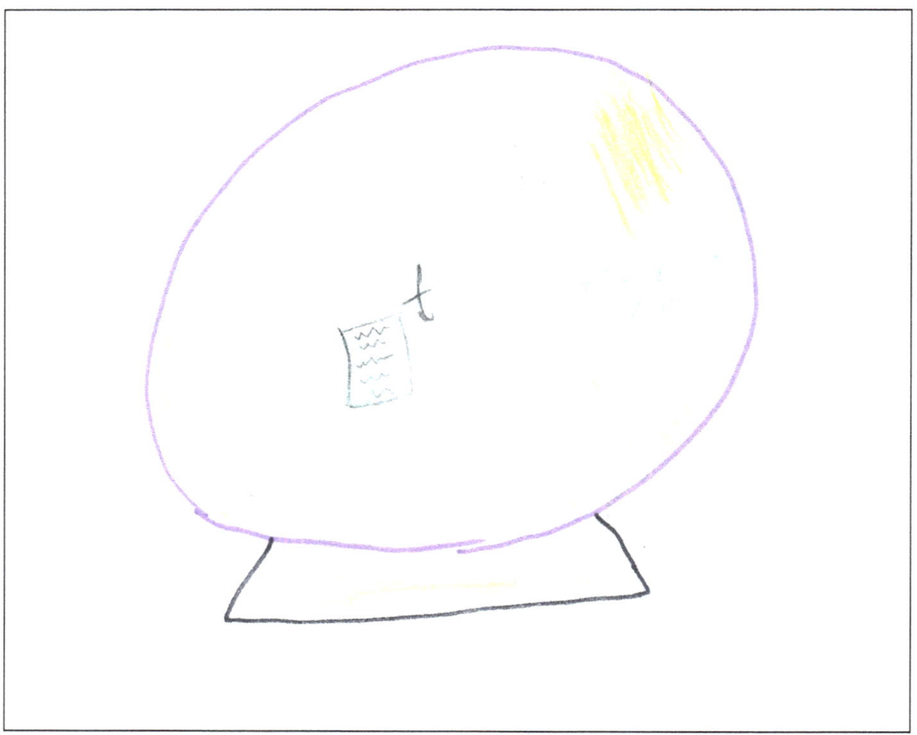

The client maintained that he could afford to make the break but that finances would be tight for a while until he could regain his financial footing.

The client, however, took a positive view about the future and his financial position because he felt that once free from the strain of his unhappy marriage he would be able to concentrate more on his work and be more productive.

This client's therapeutic intervention, therefore, concluded on an optimistic note when he was ready to face a future full of uncertainty yet with a positive and forward-looking outlook.

PRACTITIONER RESOURCES

FURTHER READING

Creative Analytical Hypnotherapy The Practitioner's Handbook by Jacquelyne Morison, Jacquelyne Morison Publishing.

Analytical Hypnotherapy Volume 1: Theoretical Principles by Jacquelyne Morison, Crown House Publishing.

Analytical Hypnotherapy Volume 2: Practical Applications by Jacquelyne Morison, Crown House Publishing.

The Truly Dynamic Therapist by Jacquelyne Morison, AuthorHouse Publishing.

FURTHER TRAINING AND DEVELOPMENT

Jacquelyne Morison is the Founder and Course Director of Jacquelyne Morison Hypnotherapy Training.

Jacquelyne Morison Hypnotherapy Training runs continuing professional development courses in Art Hypnotherapy for the qualified hypno-psychotherapeutic practitioner.

Jacquelyne Morison Hypnotherapy Training also offers full practitioner training in analytical hypno-psychotherapy which has been validated by the General Hypnotherapy Standards Council.

www.jmhypnotraining.co.uk

LIST OF CASE-STUDY EXAMPLES

INDEX